William A. Ewing

FLORA PHOTOGRAPHICA

Masterpieces of Flower Photography:
1835 to the Present

SIMON AND SCHUSTER
New York   London   Toronto   Sydney   Tokyo   Singapore

For Poyin and Charles

Half-title
DOROTHEA LANGE
Mother's Day Daisies Berkeley 1934
Silver print

Title page
DENIS BRIHAT
Black Tulip 1980
Selenium toned print

SIMON AND SCHUSTER
Simon & Schuster Building
Rockefeller Center
1230 Avenue of the Americas
New York, NY 10020

Copyright © 1991 Thames and Hudson Ltd., London

Designed by Thames and Hudson Ltd.
Typesetting by Servis Filmsetting Ltd. in Manchester, Great Britain
Printed in Singapore by C.S. Graphics Pte Ltd.

10 9 8 7 6 5 4 3 2 1

Library of Congress Cataloging-in-Publication Data

Ewing, William A.
        Flora photographica : masterpieces of flower photography : 1835 to
the present / William A. Ewing.
              p.   cm.
        ISBN 0–671–74447–X
        1. Photography of plants.   2. Flowers—Pictorial works.
    I. Title.
    TR724.E85   1991   91-8763
    779'.34—dc20   CIP

This edition is not for sale in
Great Britain or Australia.

Contents

The Flower in Photography

'A Subtlety of Vision'

In the summer of 1838 a distinguished English botanist and avid horticulturalist — a Fellow, in fact, of London's prestigious Linnaean Society — sent a breezy note to a friend who apparently shared similar passions: 'Any Cape [of Good Hope] bulbs which you have *really* to *spare*, will be very acceptable, but I consider myself not worthy of Satyriums — I was unable to flower any of those you sent before . . .'[1] The enthusiast had work of another kind on his mind as well. Writing to an Italian colleague, the botanist Antonio Bertolini, he spoke of an ingenious means by which he had *drawn* plants more perfectly than they had ever been drawn before. In truth he would have been justified in writing, 'drawn in a superhuman way', but instead claimed modestly, 'I believe that this new art will be a great help to botanists . . . especially useful for naturalists since one can copy the most difficult things with a great deal of ease . . . I have practiced this art since the year 1834.'[2] The Englishman, whose name was William Henry Fox Talbot, called his art 'photogenic drawing'; his bulb-gathering accomplice, the eminent astronomer Sir John Herschel, came up with the name which stuck — *photography*.

In the singular figure of Fox Talbot we find a pioneering photographer *and* a champion of plants. It therefore comes as no surprise to learn that 'nature's gems', as the Victorians loved to call flowers, were among the very first subjects to be pictured in photographs (**plate 24**). Admittedly, flowers were handy and expendable subject matter, especially for one who lived on a country estate with extensive gardens, but, as Talbot's biographer Gail Buckland tells us, their choice was by no means dictated solely by convenience. They were 'objects to be scrutinized in their own right. Botany was a subject of keen interest to Talbot as child and as adult . . . Perhaps more of his surviving letters refer to botany than any other subject.'[3] This is most significant, as Talbot was also an accomplished, well published, and prize-winning crystallographer, astronomer, mathematician, etymologist and Assyriologist (with no fewer than sixty published translations of cuneiform inscriptions to his credit). A quotation he chose to preface one of his books is revealing: he selected these words from the 18th-century poet and critic Joseph Warton to describe the rewards and pleasures of diligent study:

> Nor rude nor barren are the winding ways of hoar
> antiquity, but strewn with flow'rs.[4]

Talbot could not possibly have foreseen how the 'winding ways' of the path *he* had cut would themselves be 'strewn with flow'rs', but he clearly did understand that his 'sun

CI

PIONIA.

Woodcut of 'Pionia'
from *Tractatus de virtutibus herbarium*
('Herbarius Latinus' Venice 1520)

For centuries the woodcut was the sole medium for plant illustrations in *herbals*, the earliest of European printed books. Until the late Renaissance such drawings were crude and emblematic, as illustrators were in the habit of copying earlier herbals rather than drawing from nature.

Opposite: IMOGEN CUNNINGHAM
Calla late 1920s
Toned silver print

GEORG DIONYS EHRET
'Bignonia Urucu...' (Common Catalpa
Catalpa bignonioides Walt.) 1740
Gouache on vellum

This gouache demonstrates just how far botanical illustration had progressed within the span of some two hundred years. Ehret was one of the finest artists and engravers of his day. Like Franz and Ferdinand Bauer, he combined scientific discipline with an artist's eye.

JAN VAN HUYSUM (1682–1749)
Still Life of Flowers

pictures' figured within long-established tradition. It would be short-sighted to tell the story of the flower in photography as if it began abruptly in 1834. Photography *was* an invention of novel dimensions, in certain ways even a quantum leap, but it was still one end of a continuous thread, as Kenneth Clark reminds us in *Landscape into Art*:

For almost five hundred years [since the dawn of the Renaissance] artists had been applying their skill to the imitation of nature. During this time numerous methods of representation had been mastered and refined, culminating with a method which rendered light by a new combination of science and subtlety of vision.[5]

There were two distinct advantages to the new photographic method: the first concerned what Clark calls 'imitation' — the recording, or drawing function; the second concerned replication or reproduction — the communicating function. Photography in the form of Louis Daguerre's invention (the daguerreotype, which had been announced prior to Talbot's, much to his chagrin) accomplished the first function brilliantly — in many early accounts writers express their astonishment at its mirror-like fidelity — but failed miserably in the second. Talbot's method, on the other hand, fulfilled the first function adequately (though not as well as Daguerre's) and the second magnificently, as an unlimited number of positive images could be made from a single negative. This negative/positive method eventually triumphed over the one-of-a-kind daguerreotype.

In terms of the second function, photography followed in the tradition of printmaking, but with key advantages over prior media such as lithography (which had been invented less than a half-century earlier, but was dominating floral publications at the time of photography's birth), and etching, engraving and woodcut in previous times. Each medium had in turn offered greater 'subtlety of vision' — etching and engraving, with greater control over tone and line, were an improvement over woodcut, while lithography proved faster and cheaper than had etching and engraving. All these methods were highly evolved and refined, and photography, for all its advantages (the others, for example, suffered from wear on the plate), would not easily dislodge them. Moreover, those who took up photography, and those who evaluated it, expected the medium to match or better its rivals on two fronts: to produce the kinds of superlative *originals* they were used to seeing in watercolours, gouaches, pen-and-ink drawings and oil paintings, and the kinds of superlative *reproductions* they were used to seeing in lithographs, etchings and various other print media. Roger Fenton's 19th-century fruit and flower photographs, with their appropriation of 17th- and 18th-century flower painting devices, attempted to satisfy this first set of expectations (**3**), while Pietro Guidi's 19th-century photographic studies of flowering plants, modelled on standard botanical prints of the 18th century, attempted to satisfy the second (**28–31**).

This was a tall order. The painted flower piece had achieved mastery some two hundred years earlier. It had gone from a simple arrangement on the back of a 15th-century portrait by Hans Memling — a shy entry on to the stage of art history! — to paintings of such astonishing veracity that Samuel Pepys could write of a work by Herman Verelst, as early as 1669, 'The finest thing, I ever, I think, saw in my life, the drop of dew hanging in the leaves so I was forced again and again to put my finger to it to feel whether my eyes were deceived or no . . .'[6]

As for the flower print — woodcut, engraving, etching or lithograph — by the 18th century it was seen to answer 'every question that a Botanist can wish to ask, respecting the structure of the plant it represents'.[7] Goethe, introduced to the work of master illustrator Franz Bauer, claimed, 'Nature is visible, art concealed.'[8]

The traditional flower piece and the plant portrait (as botanists would call Guidi's work) are not the only genres in which there are revealing precedents in art. Doug Prince's *Transfigurations* (153) recall the fantastic flower/face hybrids of Arcimboldo. Joan Fontcuberta, who invents flowers (140), can cite the 'fleurs de fantaisie' by Jean Pillemont, or even the flowers Botticelli invented for *Primavera*.[9] David Lebe, who literally conjures up flowers out of thin air (109), reminds us of Odilon Redon's floral fictions, flowers of the mind's eye.

Photographs in which flowers are subordinate to other subject matter have also benefited from artistic precedent. When Hugo Erfurth posed the German *Neue Sachlichkeit* painter Otto Dix within a pictorial scheme which included a significant floral element (44), he was knowingly following a Renaissance model whereby painters pictured their subjects with flower arrangements which functioned as symbolic attributes, as in Hans Holbein the Younger's portrait of Thomas More, in which flowers allude to his martyrdom. In fact, in his use of the emblematic flower, Erfurth was much closer to the tradition of painting than to photography — to portray a male with the attribute of a flower was, in 1925, almost without precedent in photography.

A far more acceptable use of a floral emblem is seen in a portrait of Marlene Dietrich by Cecil Beaton (47). When Beaton personified the screen idol as a flower — moreover, of a rare and exotic variety — he was well aware of such famous precedents as Rembrandt's *Saskia as Flora* (1634), and Manet's *Olympia* (1863), the forthright study of a naked courtesan which had so enraged the French bourgeoisie; Beaton knew that the orchid behind the courtesan's ear signified lust.

Photography was born as the golden age of botanical illustration drew to a close. In the early-19th-century flower painting of Pierre Joseph Redouté, the art is said to have reached perfection — in his own day he was heralded as 'the Raphael of the Rose'. His style had a marked influence on late-19th-century photography, as we see in the work of the Reverend D. T. K. Drummond (10). More recently, the conceptual artist John Stezaker based a series of striking designs on the master's work. Now Redouté himself was one of a number of gifted specialists who had studied in Paris under the noted flower painter Gerrit van Spaendonck.[10] And he, in turn, had studied under Jan van Huysum, a late master of the Dutch flower piece. Thus, in only three or four generations, we move from the earliest painted flower pieces to the flower photography of the late 20th century.

PIERRE-JOSEPH REDOUTÉ
Bouquet of Mixed Flowers 1839
Watercolour on vellum

The golden age of botanical illlustration is said to have ended with Redouté, who carried the van Spaendonck traditions — the legacy of the Dutch flower piece, married to rigorous botanical draughtsmanship — into the 19th century. His influence can be detected in 19th-century photography.

JOHN STEZAKER
Wreath (after Redouté) 1983
Collage

Stezaker, a British conceptual artist who has made extensive use of floral imagery, has long been fascinated with Redouté's vision. He has based a series of his own images on the great illustrator's art.

'The Gems of Nature'

In one respect, William Henry Fox Talbot was not a farsighted man. He fought to restrict access to his invention through the patents he had taken out in 1841, thus hobbling the natural development of photography in England. One man who encouraged him finally to loosen his grip was the painter-turned-photographer Roger Fenton, best known to us today for his pioneering reportage of the Crimean War. Fenton devoted himself to photography for ten years, earning great distinction in the process, and just before he abandoned this activity to practice law, he undertook an extensive series of still-life studies of flowers and fruit.

The group consisted of some forty photographs, printed larger than life. The flowers and fruit were arranged on a marble table along with statuettes, bottles and pitchers of varied shape and decoration, and a touch of striped fabric or lace (3). The hand of the painter is evident: the objects are arranged precisely as they would have been by the 17th-century flower painter Wilhelm van Aelst or the early-18th-century Pieter Snyers (compare Fenton's study with this description of one of Snyer's works by Peter Mitchell: '[this] is a very casual but pleasing medley of fruit and flowers surrounding a carved ivory tankard").[11]

Across the Channel, the flower piece had its proponents, though not, perhaps, where we might first expect to find them. The daguerreotype was admirably suited to the still life (in fact, Daguerre's first work was a still life, though not of flowers), and with the French passion for flowers, floral art, and this wondrous new invention, one would expect to find many such examples. Yet still-life daguerreotypes are rare indeed — why should this be so?

Flower painting was immensely popular, and, as we have seen, had achieved extraordinary heights by 1839 in the hands of Redouté and others. The works of the Dutch masters were revered, and engravings were popular and commonplace. Daguerreotypes were by comparison tiny, and, more significantly, lacked the property of colour. But *most* significant, perhaps, was the general fascination with the human likeness. People were spellbound by the 'mirror with a memory'. There was only a supportive role for flowers as props in the form of bouquets cradled in the arms, or as arrangements on a side-table, or as bodily adornment. And as for the daguerreotypist himself, would he have been about to fritter away his time and valuable chemicals when there were clients eagerly lined up at the door for their portraits? It would have been a wealthy amateur who could have afforded to do so. Such, perhaps, was the anonymous maker of the daguerreotype presented here (12).

The finest early French examples of the flower piece appear in another medium — Talbot's calotype. Hippolyte Bayard, who had adopted the method after realizing its superiority to his own direct positive paper process (which nonetheless made him a valid third claimant to the invention of photography), loved his garden, and enjoyed staging enigmatic still-lifes there, arranging flower pots, articles of summer clothing

EUGÈNE COLLIAU
Le Mai (Watteau) 1861
Albumen print

EUGÈNE CHAUVIGNÉ
Roses and Irises c. 1877
Albumen print

and various implements against dense foliage and flowering shrubs. Flowers also play a role in one of Bayard's most charming portraits, *La Petite Boudeuse au bouquet* (not shown). But Bayard's most impressive flower picture is a magnificent still-life arrangement of flowers in a pitcher (**8**), in which he has fashioned an intricate pattern of light and shade — deep shadows curve upward from the base and metamorphose into dark blossoms, while a lighter band of blooms intersects with it; the effect of upward thrust animates the image.

Bayard might well have chosen the daguerreotype (by 1851 he was an accomplished practitioner) but instead chose the calotype, with its soft chiaroscuro. He was not alone in his preference; Henri Le Secq also produced some fine still-lifes. But generally the flower was not a priority among calotypists. Grander themes beckoned these pioneering photographers — a landscape along the Nile, the Seine at Meudon, the temple facades of Abu Simbel.[12]

Flowers came into their own in a body of work produced by a French photographer whose aims were focused on commercial and industrial applications rather than fine art. These ideas were shaped by a background in a very different field. Adolphe Braun began his career in 1831 as a fabric designer for a textile firm, and was soon involved in producing floral lithographs which could be used as source material by his fellows. The concept was not new; designers already had recourse to engravings such as Jean-Louis Prévost's *Collection des fleurs et fruits*, the stated purpose of which was 'maintaining the great French tradition for excellence of design and draughtsmanship'.[13] But Braun's idea to harness photography to the task was inspired, and by the early 1850s he was producing his reference material in the form of albumen prints. For *Fleurs photographiées*, a six-volume work of 300 plates, he selected a wide variety of field and garden flowers, arranging them in the Dutch manner as wreaths and bouquets, or scattering them randomly across the frame. Ranging from the simple to the complex, the arrangements were cleverly tailored to the needs of designers. Flowers were shown against a neutral ground, their features distinct, and when forms overlapped, care was taken not to obscure significant detail. Within a given arrangement, a specific kind of flower would be repeated, so that the designer might benefit from the variation.

Braun's efforts met with resounding success. The display of his prints at the Exposition Universelle in 1855 earned him a gold medal, and, along with *Fleurs photographiées*, accolades from the press. 'The rose seems to recover its cool incarnate . . . the finely striated iris appears to have kept its tender blue,' wrote a French reporter, while a German correspondent for the *Philadelphia Photographer* approved of the flowers' 'harmony and delicacy of modelling'.[14] But perhaps the greatest compliment came from a painter: in acknowledgment of both Braun's art and his business acumen — the success of his work abroad had allowed for the publication of an English edition of *Fleurs photographiées*, called *Flowers from Nature* — Pierre Bonnard called him 'the Nadar of flowers'.[15]

CHARLES AUBRY
Untitled c. 1860–64
Albumen print

Unlike his predecessor Adolphe Braun, Aubry was not very successful at the business of selling floral imagery as models 'from nature' for students of the fine and applied arts; he tried without success to involve the distinguished photographer Nadar in his enterprise.

CHARLES AUBRY
Untitled c. 1860–64
Albumen print

GENTILE (STUDIO), SAN FRANCISCO
Untitled
Cabinet card

A small number of photographers followed in Braun's footsteps. Arthur Martin and A. Bolotte worked together in the 1860s, along with Charles Aubry and Eugène Colliau (of whom little is known, other than his still life, '*Le Mai* (Watteau)', and a series of garden studies); and Eugène Chauvigné, a photographer established in Tours in the 1870s (**5, 7**). Like Aubry, Chauvigné may have been servicing both students of the applied *and* the fine arts with his two extensive series of floral plates. Students of painting may also have been the intended recipients of Tony Boussenot's 1860s series (**1**) and of *Still-life with Cornflowers, c.* 1870, by an anonymous photographer (**2**).

Of these photographers, perhaps the one to whom modern sensibilities are most attuned is Charles Aubry. As art historian Anne McCauley wryly observes, 'His large close-ups of isolated leaves or scattered flowers on solid grounds appeal to modern viewers who cut their teeth on Edward Weston's cabbage leaves or Imogen Cunningham's magnolias and who equate "modernism" with flatness and apparently artless minimalism, a kind of dumb frontality . . .'[16] She points out that Aubry had no aspirations to make independent artworks — his studies were designed, as Braun's had been, 'to facilitate the study of nature' by workers in the textile and fabric industries and by art students.[17] Yet this does not rule out any intrinsic aesthetic value the works may have. In Aubry's finest photographs, an acute sensibility is revealed, and the original reason for their production becomes unimportant. We are left with the work itself, not so much out of context, but within a new one — the tradition, as we know it today, of the reductivist still-life.

'Thine for Ever'

But the flower figured in far more lucrative commercial applications of photography in the 19th century. These had to do with portraiture, keepsakes of significant social occasions, especially *rites de passage* (such as funeral cards), greetings cards, tourist souvenirs, and a popular form of home entertainment: the stereograph.

The invention of the little *carte-de-visite* (playing-card size) by the French photographer Alphonse Disderi in the 1850s vastly extended the market for inexpensive portraiture.[18] One of the standard props was the floral arrangement, whether in a vase on a side-table, or held as a bouquet in the hand. These were sometimes hand-coloured in a rather cursory fashion, though they are not without a certain charm. Other conventions which, according to a report of floral photography in 1892, 'met the eye on every *carte-de-visite* [were] old favourites now grown out of fashion — to wit, the garden vase with contents and the basket filled with flowers, along with ducal pillar and balustrade'.[19] The photographer L. Caldesi produced a series of *cartes* showing wreaths of flowers, each communicating an emotional message: 'Holly — *am I forgotten?* Snapdragon — *presumption*; dahlia — *thine for ever*'. Other *cartes* were 'portraits' of individual blooms, possibly prized garden varieties brought to the studio by proud gardeners wishing to immortalize their achievements.

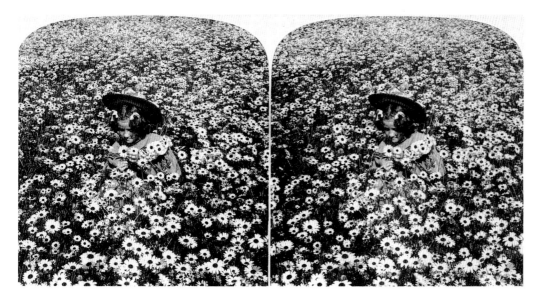

In the 1870s, or possibly earlier, photographic greetings cards with floral themes were introduced for Christmas, New Year and birthdays.[20] Flowers also featured in 19th-century mounts for photographs. The Gibson Photo Jewelry Company of Brooklyn, New York, offered floral borders to their customers in the form of photo flower medallions, photo flower clocks, photo flower plaques and birthflower medallions. The public was invited to send in treasured family portraits and choose the desired treatment from a well-stocked catalogue. In their forty years of manufacturing, Gibson's claimed to have produced more than 20 million floral medallions.[21] Apparently, surrounding a loved one with a garland of flowers functioned as a talisman.

A popular form of 19th-century entertainment was the stereograph, which provided a startling illusion of three-dimensional space. Flowers are ubiquitous in stereo, especially in the form of famous parks, gardens and conservatories (with floral clocks a favourite), and Edenesque surroundings for little children.

There was also a great market for tourists' needs, particularly for exotic flowers. Firms like Alinari in Florence (**121**), and Scowen & Co. in Ceylon (**18, 19, 66, 69**), produced high-quality prints in a variety of formats for their customers. The flowers they recorded were often unknown in Europe, or had just been introduced. The 'orchidomania' which was sweeping through Europe in the 1870s may have given Charles Scowen the motivation to record the exotic varieties he found in the botanical gardens at Peradeniya.

'The Travail of Sisyphus'

Photography was introduced just as the art of botanical illustration had reached its zenith after two hundred years of refinement.

ANONYMOUS PHOTOGRAPHER
Untitled c. 1845
Cyanotype

The cyanotype (known today as a blueprint) was invented by Talbot's friend and colleague Sir John Herschel. For the mid-19th-century botanist, the method provided a quick, simple and inexpensive alternative to the *exsicatti* and nature print.

But the draughtsmen could not keep up with the needs of the field, as botanical and horticultural publications proliferated. Drawings were time-consuming and expensive. Photography offered an obvious alternative. Yet as late as 1892 we find certain botanists pleading with their colleagues to adopt the medium:

. . . and yet a photograph of a plant in the text books is as rare as that of a human face is common. Not one out of a hundred works has confessedly availed itself of photographic aid. It is equally idle and laborious, equally burdensome and barren of satisfactory result, to search in a well-stocked library for books on botany illustrated by the camera. It is all too near akin to the travail of Sisyphus.'[22]

Excellent arguments were put forward: had not biologists used photomicrography to study insects? Had not ethnologists used photography in the field? Astronomers for the study of the sun and moon, the transit of Venus? Edward Aveling, a Fellow of University College, London, argued that 'the most rigid scientific accuracy of the hand cannot attain the absolute accuracy of photographic representation.'[23] Jules Gérard pointed out in *La Chambre noir et le microscope* that what the camera saw was 'd'une irréfutable exactitude, brutale même, excluant toute complaisance d'interprétation . . .'[24] James Mew went so far as to question the reliance on drawing, complaining that ferns 'are still represented, over and over again, by hand drawn approximate outlines of their fronds, while a few scratches, more or less artistic, are made to represent the many varieties of their complex venation'.[25] Aveling agreed: 'As things are nowadays [the 1890s] photography is not likely to be of less artistic excellence,' adding, confidently and prophetically, 'One of these days all the illustrations to botanical books will, I believe, be done by way of photography.''[26]

Yet there was fierce resistance. Teachers argued that, as a learning process, photography was no substitute for drawing. Also, photography did not have colour, 'a difficulty which we are informed by experts is likely to be long-existent, if indeed it be not everlasting'.[27] Another argument had to do with photography's specificity: a good plant drawing might incorporate parts of several different plants to end up with a truly typical specimen.

Meanwhile, there were attractive alternatives. One was the dried specimen, or *exsicatti*. Some botanists appreciated looking at nature directly. Moreover, the specimen could be dissected and studied under a microscope. Another alternative was the 'nature print', in which the plant itself was run through a press together with a soft sheet of lead, leaving an impression which (after electrotyping for strength) would hold the ink.[28] Justifying his decision to proceed with nature printing for his *Ferns of Great Britain and Ireland* in 1855, Thomas Moore stated flatly: 'The art of a Talbot or a Daguerre is insufficient.' By this he probably meant that daguerreotypes were much too small, and calotypes too indistinct.

Nevertheless, there were photographic attempts, if few and far between. As early as April 1839, Rudolph Ackermann of London advertised a 'photogenic drawing box' containing brushes, chemicals, and so on, for making one's own sun pictures. It was recommended for 'Botanists, Entomologists and the Scientific', and was 'sufficiently clear to enable ladies to practice this pleasing art'.[29] Anna Atkins, the daughter of John George Children, a distinguished scientist and colleague of Fox Talbot's, took up a photographic medium known as 'cyanotype' in 1843, by means of which she made an extensive study of British algae before turning her attentions to flowering plants (**25, 26**).[30] The cyanotype (known today as a blueprint) did not employ camera, lens, or negative, but required the practitioner merely to place an object on the photosensitive surface of the paper and expose it to light. It was, in a sense, Talbot's 'photogenic drawing', as well as a cousin of the nature print.

A decade later we find a contemporary of Charles Aubry's apparently utilizing photography in the teaching of botany. A Parisian photographer by the name of E. Reynaud, under the direction of a professor of the Lycée Louis-le-Grand, made a series of photographs showing cross-sections of flowers. The albumen prints were mounted on cards, and the various parts of each flower were clearly marked and identified (**32**).

Had they known of it, Reynaud's work would have been appreciated by botanists Aveling and Mew, but how much more delighted they would have been if the botanical photographs of the Italian Pietro Guidi had come to their attention. Here was the classic plant 'portrait', sensitively displayed with a keen eye to significant detail and hand-coloured appropriately (**28–31**).

From time to time the photographic literature of the 19th century will note an event which, unknown to the reporter, contains the seeds of a future development. One such event was the display at the Paris Exhibition of 1867 of a photographic diorama of plants from Canada, Brazil, Trinidad, Algeria and many other regions of interest for their flora. The diorama, recalled *The Photographic News* some years later, 'showed in a short space, with truth and accuracy, the principal flora of the universe',[31] and was immensely popular with the general public and photographic community alike.

ANONYMOUS PHOTOGRAPHER
Untitled n.d.
Hand-coloured tintype

'A Gossip on Floral Photography'

In the 1870s and 1880s flower studies began to appear in salon exhibitions and were reviewed enthusiastically in the periodicals. 'It is at this season of the year the artistic photographer cannot fail to be attracted by the large variety of flowers,' commented one writer, 'Photographing flowers and other small, inanimate objects is becoming more and more a favourite pastime among amateurs.'[32] Readers were told that photographing flowers cost neither the money nor the time that 'an extensive landscape practice is apt to do'.[33] After 1880 the new gelatin plates were described as a major improvement over glass, and orthochromatic film was much lauded for overcoming some of the key problems of colour. Previously, for instance, yellow and blue had required extremely long exposures even under the most favourable circumstances of light.

MARK ANTHONY
Wildflowers 1856
Collodion

Nineteenth-century art and literature was obsessed with the 'language of flowers', and to no group was the language more assiduously applied than to women and children, where flowers could be used to express youth, beauty and unsullied innocence.

The journals offered advice covering the entire process. One idea was to fix the camera overhead and lay the flowers on the floor, or on grey cardboard which, when wet, had been sprinkled with silver sand. Another writer subscribed to the overhead scheme but suggested the flowers be laid on glass above the floor, which would dispense with problematic shadows. But Mr Porrit, of the Leicester Literary and Philosophical Society, in 'A Gossip on Floral Photography', took a dim view of the overhead idea: 'Let me advise you not to adopt this plan, for it is neither dignified nor comfortable standing on a box with the neck at a painful angle, in the vain endeavour to discover what is on the screen, and to see the [lens] cap falling off into the midst of the flowers when all is ready for exposing.'[34]

A composite of these writings would give us a complete picture of the 19th-century manufacture of a conventional flower piece. Practitioners were told about focus (intentionally out-of-focus attempts, or 'fuzzytypes', were generally frowned upon); working indoors (outdoor breezes made it 'quite useless to try to obtain all [the flowers'] softness and delicacy of detail'[35]); colour ('It is still advisable to avoid, as far as possible, placing reds, blues and yellows in prominent positions . . .'[36]); lighting ('A large sheet of white cardboard should be at hand to act as a reflector to light the shadow side of the picture and to pick out the details in the interstices of the foliage . . . A short length of magnesium wire may be burnt as an auxiliary light'[37]); and exposure ('Let the mind be completely freed from all ideas of quick exposures and forced development, for such a course is absolutely and utterly impossible'[38]).

There were so many rules to follow, so many pitfalls, that many amateurs must have given up in despair. Sensing this, perhaps, the May 1887 issue of *The British Journal of Photography* held out a carrot: 'When such a line of practice is well and properly worked . . . it is quite as likely to attract the notice of the judges at the various exhibitions. . . . Witness the numerous medals which have gone to flower and similar subjects at Pall Mall and elsewhere during the past few years.'[39] And *The Photographic News* pointed out that the late great Oscar Rejlander (high priest of 'artistic photography') had regarded excellence in flower photography as the *cordon bleu* of photographic distinction.[40]

'The Mist of Dreams'

The Sunday flower photographers who were mothered along by the journals were not the only amateur photographers interested in flowers. Far more inventive schemes were devised by a group known as the Pictorialists.

From amateur clubs scattered throughout Europe, Britain and the United States, certain voices could be heard calling for a rejection of the tired conventions of the salons and a renewal of faith in photography as a legitimate, noble and unquestionably fine art. In the 1890s these voices coalesced into a chorus, singing hymns to 'composition, chiaroscuro, truth, harmony, sentiment and suggestion',[41] With their

PETER HENRY EMERSON
Gathering Water-lilies 1885
Platinum print from *Life and Landscape
on the Norfolk Broads* (1886)

Emerson offered an alternative to the manipulated
imagery of the Pictorialists. He argued forcefully and
effectively for a naturalistic approach – natural subjects in
their surroundings, photographed directly, without artistic
pretension.

emphasis on mind over mechanics, the Pictorialists sought to distance themselves from three other camps: the professionals, for whom photography was a mimetic device, and the photograph a literal transcription of reality; the old 'high-art' photographers, such as Rejlander, who sought to ape painting by building up their compositions from multiple negatives; and the growing number of snap-shooters (the Kodak had been introduced in 1888), who fired away indiscriminately at anything that caught their fancy, much as they do today.

The Pictorialists were also responding sympathetically to currents running through contemporary art and literature which questioned the primacy of fact and the omnipotence of science in the unravelling of life's mysteries. Symbolist painters and poets, following Mallarmé's dictum, '*Suggestion*, that is the dream,' looked to escape inwards, or backwards to Hellas and Parnassus. One of the leading Symbolist painters, the Belgian Fernand Khnopff, found in photography (once the print surface had been altered by his hand) another vehicle for his languid enigmas (**41**).

Pictorialists organized themselves admirably within an international network, arranged ambitious exhibitions, awarded each other medals, issued manifestos, formed alliances and generally gave each other a sense of purpose and community the likes of which had never been experienced. They questioned the very essence of the medium; they experimented with gums, oils, pigments and papers. They appropriated styles and subject-matter from painting and the graphic arts of the past and present. Negatives and prints were worked by hand so that no two finished works were alike (thus confounding critics who argued that photography was shackled to a mechanical device). Subject-matter ranged from the sublime to the ridiculous: nature, of course, in

ROBERT DEMACHY
Woman with Flowers n.d.
Gum bichromate print

Demachy was a leading French Pictorialist, well known on the international scene. The Pictorialist nude was almost inconceivable without decorative and symbolic floral accoutrements.

the form of picturesque landscapes, most often with a time-worn path or other reassuring sign of man's presence, though sometimes transformed into moonlit haunts fit for nymphs and fairies; contented mothers with happy children gambolling in flowery meadows and orchards; graceful young girls in frilly frocks sniffing delicate sprays; misty nudes entwined with exotic flowers. The function of the floral element was generally symbolic, allegorical and decorative; seldom was there any real interest in the flowers for their own sake (that is, in colour, form and texture). Artistic *arrangement* took precedence.

Baron Wilhelm von Gloeden had a penchant for classical antiquity, staging languid tableaux at his seaside villa at Taormina in Sicily. Young men and boys dressed up (or rather undressed) as Greek gods, or lute-playing shepherd boys wearing garlands or loincloths of lilies and striking Caravaggesque poses with flowers sometimes dangling from their lips (**81**). F. Holland Day, a wealthy Bostonian dilettante with an equal fondness for ancient rites (as they took shape in his fertile imagination) was more apt to use a single flower to embody an idea; in *Hypnos* (**89**) the flower appears as the very key to another reality. Sadakichi Hartmann, the foremost critic of the era, saw Day as an apostle of a more harmonious, Parnassian past. 'I know of no photographer who can drape a figure more pictorially or adorn a man's or a woman's hair with flowers in a more picturesque manner,' he wrote in *Camera Notes*, 'He likes to strike rich chords, but muffled, as it were, by the mist of his dreams.'[42]

When colour photography finally became practical with the invention of the Autochrome in 1907, pictorial photographers delighted in its painterly character. Charles Adrien (**82**) and Henri Bergon (**83**) adopted it for their studies of nudes. Edward Steichen commented: 'Personally I have no medium that can give me colour of such wonderful luminosity as the Autochrome plate. One must go to stained glass for such colour resonance . . .'[43] Heinrich Kühn, however, seems to have preferred the rich colour effects made possible by the gum-bichromate process (**16, 120**). Kühn, who enjoyed the challenge of the still life, simplified his compositions to achieve a startling immediacy, a poster-like graphic quality which sits well with modern sensibilities.

Pictorialism would eventually give way to Modernism as a dominant ethos, but the process was evolutionary, and a number of photographers can be seen as transitional figures. Kühn was one, Baron Adolf de Meyer another. A proto-modern impulse is seen in two of de Meyer's still lifes (**122, 123**). The flat spatial quality of the latter image results from the absence of a perspectival scheme, so that the glass floats in space. Its placement is also a radical departure — convention would dictate that it should sit at the bottom of the frame. Cecil Beaton once observed that de Meyer 'was not afraid of producing an almost empty photograph'.[44] But this 'emptiness' enabled him to orchestrate the patterns of reflected and retracted light. These subtleties were minutely registered in the platinum printing which de Meyer favoured.

De Meyer would never abandon Pictorialism (though this is hard to believe from the evidence of one photogram, which the viewer might well be forgiven for thinking to be by Man Ray or Moholy-Nagy) (116). Edward Steichen, on the other hand, would begin as a dedicated proponent of the misty, soft-focus school, deeply influenced by the Symbolist group known as the Nabis, and end as a determined Modernist.

Steichen had more than a casual interest in flowers. In 1906 he settled on a small farm in the village of Voulangis outside Paris and there he undertook what was to become a life-long passion for horticulture. He developed new varieties of oriental poppies, a pure blue petunia and a perennial delphinium. Soon his original three acres of cultivated flowers grew to seven, and his successful hybrids drew widespread interest, not to mention a gold medal from the National Horticultural Society of France. The coming of war, however, destroyed his hopes: 'The German cavalry scouts ride over the poppies and ride back . . . French and British soldiers pitch tents over the blue petunias and the iris,' wrote Carl Sandburg in *Steichen the Photographer*.[45] But what has survived of the garden is its spirit, in a magnificent study of heavy roses (11). This stately study of fading florescence was Steichen's lament for Europe's threatened culture.

The sad charm of *Heavy Roses* seems worlds apart from a picture Steichen made only a year later in New York. *Lotus, Mount Kisco* (74) is a paragon of Modernist virtue. Henceforth Steichen would turn his back on the moody Symbolist landscapes, portraits and nudes he had so expertly crafted. His career would take some extraordinary turns over the next decades, but he would continue to breed flowers and photograph them beautifully, often in a highly experimental vein.

EDWARD STEICHEN
Delphinium 1936
Silver print

Steichen exhibited his own prized hybrids at the Museum of Modern Art, just after he had been appointed director of the Department of Photography. 'This was the only time that living plant material had ever been shown at the Museum,' he wrote in *A Life in Photography*. 'By implication flower breeding was recognized as one of the arts.'

'Shall We Sacrifice
the Flower . . .?'

Steichen's *Lotus, Mount Kisco* might be said to mark the divide between the Pictorialist ethos and the new modern spirit which flowered between the wars. The new photography, or even 'the new vision', as a guiding spirit put it, was one of intense experiment nurtured by pre-war developments in avant-garde art, in particular Cubism, Constructivism, Dada and then, after 1924, Surrealism. While pioneering American photographers like Alfred Stieglitz and Paul Strand argued for a lucid, straightforward approach, European innovators proposed a raft of radical techniques to adequately express the dynamism of the age — oblique angles, extreme close-ups, bird's-eye and worm's-eye views, multiple exposures, photomontage, collage and cameraless imagery. Where the Pictorialists had averted their eyes from the harsh realities of the world, the new photographers embraced the chaos and intensity of urban life and the complex new technologies: 'Now the instruments of struggle are iron, concrete, steel, light and ether waves,' pronounced one German reporter,[46] while an American editor noted: 'The camera searches out the texture of flower petals and moth wings as well as the surface of concrete.'[47]

Gone are the dewy orchards, the Ophelias clutching roses, the garlanded shepherd boys. The traditional significations of the flower — purity, innocence, love and perfection — are scrupulously avoided, although the age-old associations with women and children are sometimes impossible to resist. Once flamboyant bouquets are now cut back to a single flower, or two or three. Interest is now emotionally detached and formal — a concern with form, line and texture.

Man Ray, an American transplant in Paris, was a veritable alchemist, quick to grasp the potential of new forms of photographic expression which revealed themselves as a consequence of darkroom accident — the cameraless photogram, or 'Rayograph', as he called it, and the solarization (117, 173). Flowers figure in these forms not because, as one might suppose, Man Ray had any special affection for them — he readily admitted 'taking whatever objects came to hand' — but because of their particular attributes as a class of objects. Their perfect size (as reproduction was life-size), translucence and individual variability made them ideally suited to the transformative process. What other objects could have rivalled the ragged, bursting forms in the Rayograph shown here (117)?

The photograms and solarizations quite literally 'brought to light' a dimension of objects previously undisclosed. Like other Dada iconoclasts, Man Ray believed that the artist had to eschew the literal transcription of reality in order to break through the world of surface appearances.[48] Yet to break through completely, into the realm of pure abstraction, risked losing the viewer. Man Ray was always careful to anchor his imagery in the realm of the recognizable, and flowers, which are such a vivid emblem of the real world, were the ideal anchoring device.

Far more bizarre floral elements are found in the work of other Surrealists. Hans Bellmer and George Hugnet produced imagery which lived up to De Chirico's famous declaration that art 'should always reflect a profound feeling and that profound means strange and that strange means hardly known or completely unknown' (137, 145). The Surrealists relished the opportunity to overturn the sacrosanct significations in the popular mind, subverting the old 'language of flowers' with nightmarish, perplexing visions.

Between the wars Germany was a particularly vital centre of photographic activity, and the flower asserted itself in a number of ways. The exotic flora of Sumatra were the subject of Dr Hans Shafer's documentary work in the thirties (20), while Hugo Erfurth continued to incorporate flowers (as he had done since the turn of the century) as emblems of persona into his portraiture (42, 44), and Walter Peterhans assigned flowers as exercises in tone and texture to those of his students intending to pursue careers in commercial photography and advertising (118).

The idea that plant structure was characterized by symmetry and rhythm, and that decoration and ornament should make use of stylized interpretations of plants goes back well into the 19th century. Christopher Dresser, an English botanist, had concluded in 1862 that 'all plants of a highly organized character . . . are built upon a geometric plan'.[49] Now as Owen Jones had argued a few years earlier in his dogmatic but influential *Grammar of Ornament* that 'all ornament should be based upon a geometric construction',[50] the plant was sanctified as the source *par excellence*, though it was to be interpreted and idealized as a geometric construct and not to be depicted naturalistically. And so, as conventional wisdom had it that 'photography cannot invent, as it is devoid of the mental or imaginative faculty',[51] the medium was not utilized throughout the remainder of the century in this area (with rare exceptions, one being a naturalistic floral design of an alphabet by Martin Gerlach in 1893 (119), which follows the Ruskinian ideal rather than Jones's dictates).

Although the plant reigned supreme in design for the duration of the century, it fell out of favour with the early Modernists, who opted for simple geometric patterns based on primitive cultures or the machine. Alarmed, the Art Deco designer Paul Iribe asked, 'Shall we sacrifice the flower on the altar of cubism and the machine?'[52] No!, certain photographers responded. 'Scent and colour are without doubt the beautiful thing about the plant', noted Ernst Fuhrmann in 1931, 'but the essential point, the interesting and biologically important point is the structure, and just as the external beauty is kept separate from the colour and scent, so too photography keeps this structure separate and thus allows the observer to concentrate his attentions on the essence of the plant.'[53] And Karl Blossfeldt, who, like Adolphe Braun a half-century earlier, had begun to photograph plants as an aid to designers, spoke of an even more exalted role for photography: 'The plant must be valued as a totally artistic and architectural structure. [Nature] is an educator about beauty and intrinsic feeling. My documents of plants shall promote again the unity with nature.'[54]

KARL BLOSSFELDT
Catyledon Gibbiflora 1900–1925
Silver print

Times had changed, and both Fuhrmann and Blossfeldt found a sympathetic response to their ideas. Now there was a climate which encouraged realism and scrutiny. *The World is Beautiful* were the words chosen for his book-title by Albert Renger-Patzsch, an eminent spokesman for the new vision: 'The excitement of this experience [camera vision] is that in taking a photograph the eye must adjust to a relatively small organism, like a flower; the eye must see, as it were, through the eyes of an insect, and the world as they do.'[55]

The characteristic Blossfeldt image shows a flower or plant detail taken frontally or (less often) from directly overhead. Backgrounds are neutral grey or white, and lighting is a soft, even fill which minimizes harsh shadow. Stylistically, his flower and plant forms bear a striking resemblance to the rhythmic, sinuous forms of Art Nouveau, which was the rage in Berlin when he was a student there.

Ernst Fuhrmann's photographs, both those he took himself and those he commissioned, are inseparable from his theories about the fundamental nature of life. He was a novelist and poet, not a scientist, and so his considerable imagination was not hobbled by conventional scientific wisdom. He saw life, in its plant *and* animal manifestations, as one and the same 'vital substance', evolving from one form to the other in an endless cycle of 'concentration, decomposition and new concentration'. He seems to have envisaged the animal as a plant which had 'broken away' in order to increase its potential for nourishment: '. . . roots and branches have become hands and feet and the top of the plant, the blossom, must constantly go out in search of fertile ground for nourishment.'[56]

This attitude is vividly conveyed in Fuhrmann's imagery. His plants are aggressive, searching presences, quite unlike the decorative artefacts of Blossfeldt. In our own time, when scientists are beginning to sense that there may well be something like plant 'intelligence', and our oral traditions insist on the sensitivity of plants to touch and music, Fuhrmann's ideas seem prescient.

Germany was not the only centre of European innovation in the twenties and thirties. In Czechoslovakia, for example, Karel Teige used flowers in his potent Surrealistic collages on themes of sexuality and death, while Františec Drtikol often employed flowers in his highly stylized nudes which finely balanced symbolic and expressive elements with decorative schemes derived from Cubism and Art Deco (90). Here the flower arrangement is a cipher of the body's voluptuousness — the bloom of breast and thigh.

From France alone we might gather a fine bouquet of floral photographs. The brothers Jean and Pierre Auradon continued in the grand still-life tradition of Braun and Aubry, while Emmanuel Sougez adopted a spare Modernist style of studio work (75). Sougez's artful designs were poles apart from the naturalistic documents of his countryman, the renowned Eugène Atget (160). Atget, who photographed flowers within the larger context of a vast documentary project on Paris and its environs between 1896 and 1923, showed his subjects in their natural surroundings of parks and gardens. In his more formal studies of the great gardens of Versailles, St Cloud and the like, the flowers are simply elements of grandiose garden design, of less interest in themselves than the trees, lawns, architecture and ornament. But within the context of informal schemes — such as private gardens — waterlilies, poppies and varieties of roses are depicted with affection. Often Atget included a comforting sign of a nurturing human presence — a trellis, garden implements, an old wicker chair — recalling the rustic charm of that first French garden study by Hippolyte Bayard.

'Good, Plain Pictures'

The arrival in America of the new European photography in the twenties and thirties in the form of intelligent and comprehensive museum exhibitions, was greeted with qualified enthusiasm. The American Realist school, founded by Eakins and Homer and typified by the 'good, plain pictures' of Charles Sheeler, Paul Strand, Walker Evans and Alfred Stieglitz, could embrace the lucid documentary work of Albert Renger-Patzsch, but the more radical inventions of László Moholy-Nagy and Man Ray (now more of a European than an American!) were greeted with some skepticism and hostility. Nevertheless, American photographers welcomed the chance to see what their European counterparts were up to, and in landmark exhibitions, such as 'International Photographers' held at the Brooklyn Museum in 1932, the major American Modernists hung side by side with the best from Europe. Some of the most striking pictures were those of plants and flowers.

Charles Sheeler was already well informed about advanced European art when he took up the camera in 1910. 'Good art has got to be in the thread of the great tradition,' he concluded, 'An underlying current goes through all the way to Renaissance, Egyptian, Chinese, back to cave painting.'[57] He decided that Cubism (by which he meant rigorous analysis) was 'the ultimate discipline' and crafted a simplified form of it in his own painting and photography, stressing a fundamental geometry, shallow space and flattened perspective. *Zinnia and Nasturtium Leaves* is a masterpiece of significant form (**124**); its spare geometry was undoubtedly inspired by the austere Shaker architecture he was photographing at the time.

Another important American whose work hung at Brooklyn was Paul Outerbridge. Though he, too, had been influenced by Cubism and abstraction, it was Surrealism which held him in thrall. 'Art is life seen through man's craving for perfection and beauty', he wrote late in his life, '— his escape from the sordid realities of life into a world of his imagination.'[58] Flowers seem to have been one means of escape, or at least a buffer from those realities. They appear along with his many highly erotic nudes, strewn on the ground or held in bouquets (**93, 95**). Outerbridge would say nothing to cast light on these enigmas, declaring that 'higher art forms exist for themselves alone and do not need another art form to enhance their significance.'[59]

IMOGEN CUNNINGHAM
Two Callas c. 1929
Silver print

Among the best known of 20th-century flower photographers, Cunningham was able to strike a balance between her geometric design sense and naturalism.

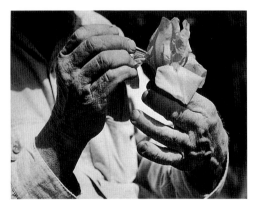

ALMA LAVENSON
Hands of the Iris Breeder 1932
Silver print

Also represented in the Brooklyn exhibition was a contingent from the west coast, led by Edward Weston and Imogen Cunningham, renegade Pictorialists who, along with a small group of like-minded photographers, had banded together informally under the banner *F64* in order to champion what Weston called 'pure photography — unaided by the hand', and 'The Thing itself . . . the quintessence revealed direct.'[60] For Weston himself, 'The Thing' did not often include the flower. Perhaps he avoided them because they were so much a part of the Pictorialist's stock-in-trade, and traditional sentiment wrapped them too tightly in its folds. With his famous pepper, on the other hand, he had found an object which was free of such associations, and he was free to suggest new ones. No one would have been excited by an eroticized rose, but an eroticized pepper was a revelation. When Weston *did* photograph flowers, the old sentimentality was dramatically exorcised (**183**).

Just as the Americans showed an interest in their European colleagues, the Europeans followed American developments. Along with Steichen, Weston had been asked to select the American contribution to a major international showing held in Stuttgart in 1929. *Film und Foto*, or 'Fifo' as it was affectionately known, brought together the major talents on both sides of the Atlantic — Man Ray, Kertész, Moholy-Nagy, Renger-Patzsch, Blossfeldt, Sheeler, Steichen, Outerbridge, Weston, and, along with other American notables, Imogen Cunningham, whose flowers and plants had excited Weston only the year before.[61]

Flowers and plants had been an interest of Cunningham's at least since 1910, when she had opened her studio in Seattle, posing her sitters next to pots of Chinese lilies, or taking them outside into the garden. All her life botany and horticulture remained important to her and she counted among her dearest friends botanists and gardeners who brought her exotics to photograph or plant in her own garden.

She had a keen appreciation of plant architecture and a singular sense of composition. Many flower photographers have been defeated by massed foliage, finding it impossible to resolve as form. But not Cunningham, who had a great talent for animating line and contrasting tone. She played the tonal range like a virtuoso, using light like a chisel. Her works border on abstraction but do not succumb to it, finding a satisfying tension (as we see in *Magnolia Blossom,* **77**) between abstraction and representation. Nor are her flowers mute, merely formal exercises, but full of suggestion, sexual and otherwise — the legacy, perhaps, of her Pictorialist years.

There were others of Cunningham's generation who focused to varying degrees on the subject of the flower. Close in interest and friendship was Alma Lavenson (**71**), who illustrated books and articles for the horticulturalist Sidney Mitchell (whose 'portrait' is seen in *Hands of the Iris Breeder*). Ansel Adams, popularly associated with the great western vista, made a number of fine studies of flowers in their natural settings which continued in the tradition of Paul Strand's photographs of vegetation begun in 1925. The Adams image reproduced here, therefore, is atypical, demonstrating more of a kinship with Weston and Cunningham (**177**).

Konrad Cramer brought to his flower photographs a non-objective painter's love of abstraction (64); when he focused closely on the flower it was not to reveal plant structure, but to probe beyond it. 'Longing for "reality"', he wrote to Steichen, '– not the reality of objects, but the reality of surface, light and texture . . .'[62] Francis Bruguière (114) was also obsessed with abstraction as a means of inner vision, but whereas Cramer achieved his end by means of extreme close-up, Bruguière achieves his through a kaleidoscopic multiple exposure.

'X-ray Goes Pictorial

The first decades of the 20th century also saw progress in botany. The artist's 'Rayograph' had its counterpart in the scientist's 'radiograph', or X-ray. Radiography was invented in 1895, but not until 1912 do we hear of an X-rayed flower. This honour belongs to Pierre Goby, who exhibited his imagery at the Royal Photographic Society in the following year. In 1914 J. Hall-Edwards published an excellent X-ray of tulips. The botanist now had a means of revealing the interior structure of flowers without the need for dissection, while 'the periodic radiography of a growing plant . . . opens up a field of great value to the naturalist'.[63] Scientific literature of the twenties and thirties also includes suggestions as to aesthetic applications of the technique. One writer, unknowingly invoking a tradition going back to Adolphe Braun in the 1850s, wondered if designers might not use the imagery to develop stylized motifs! Dr Dain Tasker wrote

× 10

1. One by one the anthers open and shed their pollen.

2. The flower teems with pollen, but the hidden stigmas are unable to receive it. Already the topmost anthers are empty (their broken walls can now be seen).

3. All the anthers are withered and from the axis of the

column the style elongates out. The stigmas project out of the top.

4. Finally, the tuft expands into a whorl of stigmas. It is ready to receive the pollen, but the flower itself does not now possess any.

The pollen of the mallow, like that of the white campion, must be carried from the male flowers (the young flower) to the female flowers (the older flower).

× 10

. . . *is first male*

and later female.

42

43

Pages from R. H. NOAILLES
The Hidden Life of Flowers
trs. J. M. Guilcher, London, 1954

For all its promise, photography was not adopted by 19th-century botanists. Not until well into the 20th century do we find the medium irrevocably entrenched in the field.

an upbeat article for *Popular Photography* called 'X-ray Goes Pictorial', and his own lyrical examples were forceful evidence (**180**).[64]

By the early years of the 20th century, botanical or naturalistic photographers were also making great strides. E. T. Harper was a botanist, clergyman and mycologist who took numerous photographs, apparently over decades (**21**). Henry Troth was a Pictorialist who was somehow able to put aside his artistic yearnings when it came to the photography of the flowers he loved; his studies have a sense of vitality and wholeness quite unlike the detached and clinical work of Harper (**22**). Edwin Hale Lincoln undertook, over a period of thirty years, what is possibly the most extensive photographic project ever involving flowers. His *Wildflowers of New England*, published as a limited edition portfolio of platinum prints in 1910, comprises some four hundred plants, some of which were photographed outdoors (requiring him to wait patiently for hours for the right play of light), while many of which were taken indoors, roots and all, and expertly arranged and lit to suggest their natural habitat (**73**). Sensitive to potential damage by human predators, he never disclosed the locations of what he liked to call his 'friends'.

And finally there was response to Edward Aveling's late-19th-century pleas for photography to be harnessed to botanical publications. Books and journals shifted inexorably from hand-drawn imagery to photography during the twenties and thirties. Yet the full potential was not realized until mid-century, when books began to be published in which photographs were the equal of the text. 'One can say that the very soul of the flower has been caught on the negative,' reads the preface to R. H. Noailles' *The Hidden Life of Flowers* (1954), a model of photographic enlightenment: 'With the help of photography these processes are brought right before the reader's eyes. This, then, is the method proposed: to study an illustration in detail, to compare it with other pictures and draw conclusions from the comparison. *The inclusion of a text is merely a preparation, guide and completion of this essentially personal activity on the part of the reader*' (author's italics).[65]

Multiplicity and Possibility

In the annals of documentary photography we find a cornucopia of 'flower photographs': images in which flowers play a significant, though not necessarily a central, role in a broader social or cultural scheme. Rare indeed is the documentarian, photojournalist or independent street photographer who does not have a dozen such pictures in his or her oeuvre. In this genre flowers appear as commodities, ornaments and in various symbolic guises (as tokens of love and affection, as emblems, talismans and even omens).

For Lewis Hine early in the 20th century, the significance of the flower was social and economic, its status that of a commodity, the manufacture of which provided a tenuous livelihood for struggling American immigrant familes. But for Louis Faurer, working at

LEWIS HINE
Family Making Artificial Flowers c. 1910
Silver print

ANTON BRUEHL
Untitled c. 1935
Toned silver print

The flower seller, the flower girl, the florist's shop . . . these are enduring themes in documentary photography.

mid-century, it was something more; bought and sold by literally faceless cityfolk (166), it was a point of human contact in a sea of urban anonymity.

Other recurring 'commodity' themes in documentary photography include the flower girl, the flower vendor with cart or stall, and the florist's shop window, all of which are found in numerous 19th- and 20th-century examples (163).

In the venerable documentary tradition of street photography we find varied significations of the flower. For Jerome Liebling (164) a flower arrangement spied in a Spanish shop window, neatly equated with a communion dress, stands for respectful tradition and orderly social life. For Josef Sudek (170), a withered bouquet found on a gravestone in Prague's Mala Strana cemetery is a poignant token of love. And for Helen Levitt (52), Izis (168) and Louis Faurer (53), the flower is an emblem of what is always at risk in the city – delicacy, tenderness and hope.

A younger generation of street photographers has been less willing to accept the traditional association of the flower with unsullied nature, or with true escape from the dehumanizing urban milieu. For photographers like Kenneth Josephson (167), Joel Meyerowitz and Robert Walker (163), the flower is an emblem of pathos. In their work artificial flowers thrive in ludicrous environments and are fashioned into outrageous decorative schemes, while real ones wither away behind glass or are forced into undignified poses to conform to some urbanite's idealized conception of nature.

The flower *in* nature has become another ambivalent subject in recent decades. Partly in revulsion to the prettified, escapist scenes of commercial photographers, which gloss over the untold damage we have wrought on our environment, the nature photographer has tended to shy away from the flower and concentrate on more encompassing vistas which do show the hand of man.

Early in the century – perhaps even to mid-century – it was possible for photographers to believe in nature and to find and express a boundless joy in it. In America, for instance, Paul Strand could find such a moment in a cluster of wildflowers in a rocky crevice; William Giles's *Calla Lily, Oregon* (176) is also in this tradition. In Europe, Edwin Smith fashioned images of the English countryside with Ruskinian charm (172), while Denis Brihat photographed with great affection the cherry trees near his home in the south of France (161), speaking of them as his 'friends . . . – it was fine to meet them several times a year'.[66] But today's photographer approaches nature warily. He or she is likely to subvert the greetings card sentimentality with signs of nature's desecration – trash, oil slicks on water, jet trails or overhead wires in the sky. Barbara Crane finds her own method of subversion in her startling series, 'Visions of Enarc' (147); through the use of extreme close-ups from a worm's-eye perspective and blinding flash, Crane's flowers take on a wholly unfamiliar, even monstrous, character – reminders of man's insufficient understanding of the vegetal world, or omens portending some catastrophe of nature.

On the other hand, the cultivated flower, the flower of gardens, parks and yards, tends to be a more comfortable tradition, perhaps because the culture of the park and

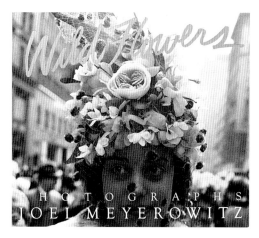

Front cover of JOEL MEYEROWITZ
Wildflowers New York 1983

Meyerowitz's book was a compilation of photographs he had taken over the years in which a flower (or flowers) or floral motif was a significant though not necessarily central element of the picture. What strikes the reader is the ubiquity of floral imagery in everyday life, its hold on the human mind even as our lives are increasingly distanced from nature.

PAUL STRAND
The Happy Family, Orgeval, France 1958
Silver print

garden remains intact and unthreatened. Some of the finest recent work in this genre has been accomplished by Lee Friedlander (**171**), who makes a virtue of dense and layered subject matter, rewarding the viewer who pays close attention to the finely nuanced forms and tones. Yet for all the image density, Friedlander is always careful to maintain the flower's integrity — it is never distorted or abstracted. 'You have to be responsible to the subject,' he argues, 'A flower can't look like concrete.'[67]

Since Imogen Cunningham's day, the lure of the reductivist still-life has proven irresistible to many photographers. There is a quite extraordinary diversity of approaches to what is, after all, somewhat restricted subject matter. Some photographers, such as E. F. Kitchen (**76**) and Dr Albert G. Richards (**40**), work with the whole flower, while others, Yasuhiro Ishimoto (**59**), for example, isolate a fragment which stands for the whole. Ishimoto employs an extreme close-up of a petal, stopping short, however, of complete abstraction; beyond a certain point, as with John Atchley's deep penetration to the heart of a flower (**61**), the image transports the viewer away from representation into the realm of abstraction and suggestion.

In recent years a new sphere of exploration has opened up: the dead and dying flower. Chris Enos (**68, 181**), Cay Lang (**67**) and Barbara Norfleet (**182**) recognized that their choice of subject matter would disturb those people who cannot or do not wish to see beyond the flower's traditional signification of unsullied beauty, perfection and vitality, and would confound those critics who (making the same assumptions) dismissed the flower as a subject worthy of *serious* photography. In any event, the physical characteristics and behaviour of dying flowers were found to be very different from those of living ones. The shrinking and shrivelling, wilting and withering dramatically transformed every property and therefore revealed a whole new aesthetic terrain. There is a certain majesty to these images of valiant struggle. Seen in this light, the expiry of Lang's *Ophelia* takes on a heroic aspect.

The tradition of the flower arrangement, the flower piece, has not lost its appeal over the years. Rosalind Maingot's lush study of peonies (**131**) is a fine example of the resilience of Dutch 17th-century conventions, while Sheila Metzner's highly stylized still-lifes look back to Art Nouveau, Art Deco and the asymmetrical compositions of oriental flower painting (**133**).

Nature is not acknowledged in Metzner's dreamy imagery. The origins of her exotics in jungle habitats have long been forgotten in their forced march to distant cities; the flowers have been thoroughly acculturated. The same may be said of Robert Mapplethorpe's elegant, theatrical arrangements (**50, 127, 175**). For both photographers the flowers are cultural artefacts, valued for their rarity, design and aristocratic rank among their own kind, as is the fine glassware which contains them. The flower is an emblem of privilege, refinement and exclusion, like *haute couture* in fashion magazines. But whereas Metzner's flowers are languid, passive creatures, Mapplethorpe's are aggressive, jutting sexual presences: an extension of human flesh and blood — an equation vividly clear in a self-portrait of sorts (**50**).

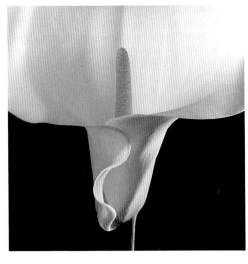

ROBERT MAPPLETHORPE
Calla Lily 1988
Silver print

Mapplethorpe's work is often compared with Cunningham's. Cunningham, however, was interested in the flower as a natural being, the flower in conjunction with the plant, whereas Mapplethorpe had no such interest — for him the flower was, in a sense, more of a man-made object.

Where Mapplethorpe simplifies and refines, Steve Lovi (135) and Don Worth (132) make a virtue of complexity and illusion. Worth, for example, relies for his *trompe l'oeil* effect on a ground of densely printed floral fabric into which are 'woven' real flowers and objects, the patterns and textures of which correspond to their printed cousins. Worth's study owes its oriental character only partially to the fabric; the manner in which the items are arranged recalls 17th-century Chinese woodcuts in ink and watercolour.

A different tradition is also invoked in Jan Groover's enigmatic still-life (125), perhaps the most minimal of 'fruit and flower pieces', poles apart from — but on the same continuum as — Roger Fenton's sumptuous 19th-century display (3).

What are we to make of this iconography? Groover is on record as saying, 'formalism is everything,' so is this merely a formal exercise?[68] Perhaps not; read with the traditional significance of the objects depicted, the image is as morally instructive as the 17th-century allegorical flower painting of Matthias Woos — the Greek column representing, on one level, the resolution of form, on another the flowering of civilization; this in turn is the basis for aesthetic contemplation, represented by the cut (i.e., domesticated) flower, while the fruit signifies bodily nourishment; thus a harmony of mind and body.

A deep reverence for nature and culture also pervades the personal iconography of Olivia Parker (113). Her lyrical still-lifes juxtapose flowers with segments of architectural drawings and newspapers, bits of discarded metal, gems, the workings of old clocks and other found objects which signify the flower of human enterprise. Less reverential — of culture, at least — are the garish arrangements of Brian Ogglesbee (148), which mock the tasteless ostentation characteristic of arrangements in hotel lobbies and funeral homes, and the exaggerated colour effects associated with advertising photography.

Contemporary photographers continue to explore, or propose, relationships between the flower and the human body. Michael Spano suggests the flower as a sixth sense, attuned to intimations which otherwise go unheard (48), while Sally Mann festoons a child's legs with a sinuous arrangement of gooseneck loosestrife in a rhythmic dance of fluid form (88).

The flower also continues to do service as an emblem of persona. Photographers have found that artists are particularly willing collaborators when it comes to their portraits. The actress Foun Sen takes on the countenance of a rose for Raymond Voinquel (49), while Salvador Dali does his best to discredit reality for Jean Dieuzaide (55) and Lucas Samaras willingly dematerializes behind his own floral shirt at the suggestion of Arnold Newman (57).

Apparently deeply rooted in the psyche is the floral symbolism of desire. Bert Stern caught a latter-day Venus, the actress Marilyn Monroe, in a provocative pose, holding overblown roses — traditional attributes of the goddess of love — to her breasts (91). But roses have thorns, as Eikoh Hosoe reminds us in *Barakei* (Ordeal by

Roses), a series of surreal tableaux in which the renowned writer/actor Yukio Mishima journeys through a dreamscape of memory and desire (**54**). For Elisabeth Sunday, visions also sprout from the soil of dreams (**96–98**). Her figure and flower diptychs and triptychs are, however, a heaven to Hosoe's hell; their message is one of release, not trial.

'The Comfort of Frames'

Photographers have never been content to restrict themselves to the flowers of the real world, as 19th-century fabrications testify (**138, 139**). Counting on the viewer's uncritical faith in the photograph's veracity, Joan Fontcuberta masks his deceptions by appropriating the dispassionate 'scientific' style of botanical photography (**140, 141**). With monstrous grafts he mocks the most sacred of *flora photographica*, the calla lily and the bird of paradise. These are the most literal examples of what we might call photographic hybrids (or, in their most disturbing form, mutations), imagery in which the flower is cultivated, so to speak, in the mind. In such pictures the flower itself may be less the true subject than the medium in which it is depicted. For Doug and Mike Starn, for instance (**107**), the rose is a useful icon because of its emblematic ambiguity (mystery, secrecy, love, etc.), but it is not of intrinsic interest — their iconoclastic tearing and taping (of an object we are used to seeing whole) sees to that. Such images are intended to question and extend photographic syntax, and thereby perception itself.

The hybrids and mutations are therefore of two types: those in which the *flowers* are invented, or transformed with photographic tools and techniques; and those in which the *image* itself is the hybrid, in the form of a composite.

A number of photographers have chosen the first course. Suzanne Opton (**115**) for instance, intervenes in the subject matter, isolating the individual blossoms of gladioli with small pieces of paper and creating an illusion of a multiplicity of still lifes within a single frame. Marvin Gasoi also intervenes, but he does so in the photographic process, literally painting the flowers with neonesque light during the long time-exposures (**104**); the exotic forms of the anthurium ('painter's palette') and bird of paradise provide Gasoi with a basic pattern and colour scheme which he elaborates and intensifies. David Lebe also paints with light, but his flowers (in this particular example, **109**) are conjured out of thin air. However, Lebe grounds his imagination in reality (in the form of the vase, table and floor); in this way, the viewer is led to believe that he is seeing reality afresh rather than a pure figment of the artist's imagination.

The range of composite imagery is considerable, as individual artists like John Stezaker and Gordon L. Bennett (**142, 112**) work with and extend traditional photomontage and collage, or craft new forms by combining two or more negatives, transparencies or prints, as do Jerry Uelsmann, Doug Prince and Pierre Boogaerts, among others (**155, 154, 110**). 'Oh, the comfort of frames,' writes Pierre Boogaerts in a vigorous attack on the complacency with which we view the single frame: '[We] never address the exterior. Never what is missing from the image, what connects the rectangle to the exterior, or, quite simply, to the film, the mechanism, or to the tooled gaze of the lenses.'[69]

Consideration of a final and somewhat different type of composite, or hybrid, takes us back to that moment, more than one hundred and fifty years ago, when François Arago dazzled his listeners with a vision of photography's transcriptive powers:

To copy the thousands of hieroglyphs covering even the exteriors of the great monuments of Thebes, Memphis and Karnak, etc., would require scores of years and legions of draftsmen. One single man could carry out this task using the daguerreotype.[70]

Yet a hundred and fifty years later, this fantasy, now realized, has lost its lustre. The whole world, it seems, has had to submit to being copied. This surfeit, and our own jaded response to it, is both subject and subject matter of Rick Hock's unique brand of assemblage, the *Codex*, of which *Natural History* (111) is one of a continuing and extensive series.

Hock's grid assemblies consist of previously published material, unearthed, as it were, from encyclopaedias, textbooks, brochures, magazines — in short, from the mass of photographic imagery that is beamed at us daily. For this particular composite Hock has appropriated as major components the floral X-rays of Dr Albert G. Richards (40) and the electron scannings of flowers and insects by David Scharf. But for Hock, the *specimen* is not — as it was for Richards and Scharf — the flower itself, but rather the way Richards and Scharf look at the flower. In this transfiguration, locked into a grid which seems to connote some rigorous, 19th-century classificatory scheme, their flowers lose their ethereal beauty and take on a monstrous aspect, like mutations from some nuclear catastrophe or accident.

Our uncertain relationship with nature is also the theme of Victor Landweber's witty composite, *Flower Garden* (149),in which the flower beds, so to speak, consist of paint chips the artist has collected and laid in neat rows in the manner of typical colour charts. The captions, also 'found', resonate with melodramatic tones which a Victorian would appreciate (as if to make up for the dispirited display) — 'Imperial Rose', 'Withered Rose', 'Vivid Violet'. Nature, Landweber implies, has not only been irretrievably lost to us, but even the ideal has been desecrated.

Will the flower persevere? Photography may be one end of a continuous thread of pictorial representation stretching back to antiquity, but one day this link will be the *penultimate* one, superseded by a medium hitherto inconceivable. Then the 20th century will be seen as the era of the photograph, as the 19th century was seen as the era of the lithograph, and the Middle Ages that of the woodcut. Most likely the flower *will* preserve its tenacious hold on our imagination, envoy of Ruskin's 'mysteries and presences innumerable'.[71] The flower will appear in guises wholly new yet somehow familiar, that familiarity due in no small measure to the inventive photography of the past 150 years from which it will naturally evolve.

Bloom

'At this season of the year the artistic photographer cannot fail to be attracted by the large variety of flowers, many of which are exceedingly suitable, both in shape and colour, to form charming subjects for photographic treatment.'
The Photographic News, July, 1885

The flower piece, a pleasing arrangement of cut flowers in a vase, usually in the form of a radial composition, came into its own in the 17th century in the hands of Dutch and Flemish painters. Ever since, the attraction of lush, full-blown flowers at the peak of their bloom - with their traditional associations of beauty, vitality and perfection - has continued undiminished. When photography arrived at the mid -19th century, early practitioners such as England's Roger Fenton (a painter turned photographer) and Hippolyte Bayard in France were quick to adopt the medium for the flower piece. But there were other photographers for whom the new medium was not a question of art for its own sake. Some entrepreneurs seized upon the idea of floral photography for greetings cards, often hand-coloured 'with a brilliance rivalling nature', according to one contemporary journal, while others, like Adolphe Braun and Charles Aubry, set up businesses to manufacture models for students of the applied and fine arts. Amateurs were encouraged to take up 'floral delineation' as an inexpensive alternative to landscape practice, while inventors such as the Lumière brothers found in the flower piece a perfect showcase for their technical achievements in colour photography. One hundred years after the first monochrome flower pieces appeared in the form of daguerreotypes and calotypes, the fruits of all these labours, both scientific and aesthetic, would combine in the superlative colour prints of Edward Steichen, photographer and horticulturalist, who focused his lens on his own hybrid delphiniums.

1 TONY BOUSSENOT
Flowers 1860s
Albumen print

2 ANONYMOUS FRENCH PHOTOGRAPHER
Still Life with Cornflowers c. 1870
Albumen print

3 ROGER FENTON
Fruit and Flowers 1860
Albumen print

4 ADOLPHE BRAUN
Flowers c. 1853
Albumen print

5 EUGÈNE CHAUVIGNÉ
Camellias, No. 24 c. 1877
Albumen print

6 CHARLES AUBRY
Flowers c. 1860—64
Albumen print

7 EUGÈNE CHAUVIGNÉ
Untitled, No. 6 c. 1877
Albumen print

8 HIPPOLYTE BAYARD
Vase of Flowers 1842–50
Calotype

9 FREDERICK HOLLYER
Lilies after 1870
Platinum print

10 REVEREND D. T. K. DRUMMOND
Untitled c. 1860
Albumen print

11 EDWARD STEICHEN
Heavy Roses, Voulangis, France 1914
Silver print

12   ANONYMOUS FRENCH (?) PHOTOGRAPHER
Still Life c. 1845
Daguerreotype

13 AUGUSTE and LOUIS LUMIÈRE
Lilacs 1907
Autochrome plate

14 EDWARD STEICHEN
Delphiniums 1940
Process-dye imbibition

15 EDWARD STEICHEN
Untitled c. 1910
Autochrome plate

16 HEINRICH KÜHN
Phlox after 1904
Oil transfer print on tissue

Enquiry

'Well after Redouté, scientific curiosity carried the pursuit of plant sensibility much further. A system of veins and nerves, pulses and voluntary movements appear in plants. Beneath the lenticular eye the secrets of the flower fall one by one . . . '

Colette, 'Secrets', *Prisons et Paradis,* 1932

The earliest published account of an attempt at photography, by Humphry Davy in 1802, tells us that a botanical subject was employed. William Henry Fox Talbot likewise used flowers and leaves for his 'photogenic drawing', informing his botanist colleagues of the new medium's advantages over drawing by hand. Anna Atkins, the world's first woman photographer, working with her friend Ann Dixon, settled on a photographic method devised by Sir John Herschel called cyanotype, finding it preferable to the established procedures of the mounted specimen and the nature print.

Yet for all the good arguments put forward, photography was ignored by botanists in the 19th century. 'A photograph in the text-books is as rare as that of a human face is common,' reported *The Photographic News* in April 1892. The studio work of E. Reynaud and Pietro Guidi, therefore, and the field work of Scowen & Co. and William Stillman, must count as rare exceptions rather than the rule. Not until the turn of the century did the extensive photographic plant survey come into its own, and not until the 1920s and 1930s, in the works of Karl Blossfeldt and Ernst Fuhrmann, was it widely communicated.

Enquiries are not always botanical: Louis Ducos du Hauron's quest was for a practicable method of colour photography, and a flower merely served his purpose, while Dr Albert G. Richards utilized the X-ray with aesthetic, rather than scientific, revelation in mind.

17 ANONYMOUS PHOTOGRAPHER
Heliconia Barqueta (False Plantain; Model) *c.* 1930–40
Silver print

CORYPHA UMBRACULIFERA.
TALIPOT PALM IN FLOWER.

CORYPHA UMBRACULIFERA.
THE LAST STAGE OF THE TALIPOT.

18, 19 SCOWEN & CO.
Corypha Umbraculifera (Talipot Palm) in Flower (top);
The Last Stage of the Talipot c. 1870s
Albumen prints

20 DR HANS SHAFER
Amorphophallus Brooksii, Lebong, Sumatra 1937
Copy print from journal

21 EDWARD THOMSON HARPER
Camassia Scillida (Camas) c. 1920
Silver print

22 HENRY TROTH
Sarracenia Purpurea (Pitcher-plant) c. 1900
Silver print

23 ANONYMOUS PHOTOGRAPHER
Sanguinaria Canadensis ('Bloodroot') *c.* 1930—40
Silver print

24 WILLIAM HENRY FOX TALBOT
Photogenic Drawing 1835 or 1839–40
Salted-paper print

Cypripedium
(*Portland ...*)

Trichromie rétrospective — Anciens essais.
Feuilles et pétales de fleurs par contact, 1869.

Louis Ducos du Hauron

25, 26 ANNA ATKINS and ANN DIXON
Cypripedium Acaule (Pink Lady's Slipper) Collected in Portland, Maine 1854 (top)
Trillium Erectum, Bangor, Maine   c. 1850 (bottom)
Cyanotypes

27 LOUIS DUCOS DU HAURON
Trichromie rétrospective — Anciens essais. Feuilles et pétales de fleurs par contact 1869
Three-colour carbon assembly print

Orchis tephrosanthos Will.

Sanremo prati di Bignone

Fiorisce in Maggio.

F. Panizzi Botanico Direttore.   P. Guidi Fotografo.

Convolvulus arvensis L.

Sanremo, luoghi incolti.

Fiorisce tutta l'estate.

F. Panizzi Botanico Direttore.   P. Guidi Fotografo.

Ophrys aranifera Huds.

Arma di Taggia, presso il forte

Fiorisce in maggio

F. Panizzi Botanico Direttore.   P. Guidi Fotografo.

Sternbergia lutea Ker. et S.

Sanremo alle siepi

Fiorisce da ottobre a novembre

F. Panizzi Botanico Direttore.   P. Guidi Fotografo.

28–31 PIETRO GUIDI
Botanical Studies 1870s
Albumen prints with hand-colouring

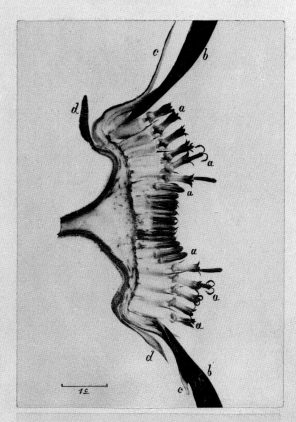

FAMILLE DES COMPOSÉES
SOLEIL ANNUEL (Helianthus annuus)
TRANCHE VERTICALE DU RÉCEPTACLE DES FLEURS
a, fleurons à divers degrés de floraison
b, demi fleuron   c, bractées de l'involucre
d, bractées de la base de l'involucre

A Paris, chez E. Reynaud, Rue du Faubourg Poissonnière, 134
Déposé

32 E. REYNAUD
Familles des composées, soleil annuel
(Helianthus Annuus) before 1863
Albumen print

33 WILLIAM JAMES STILLMAN
Untitled c. 1880
Albumen print

34 KARL BLOSSFELDT
Phacelea Tanacetifolia 1900—25
Silver print

35 KARL BLOSSFELDT
Tellima Grandiflora 1900—25
Silver print

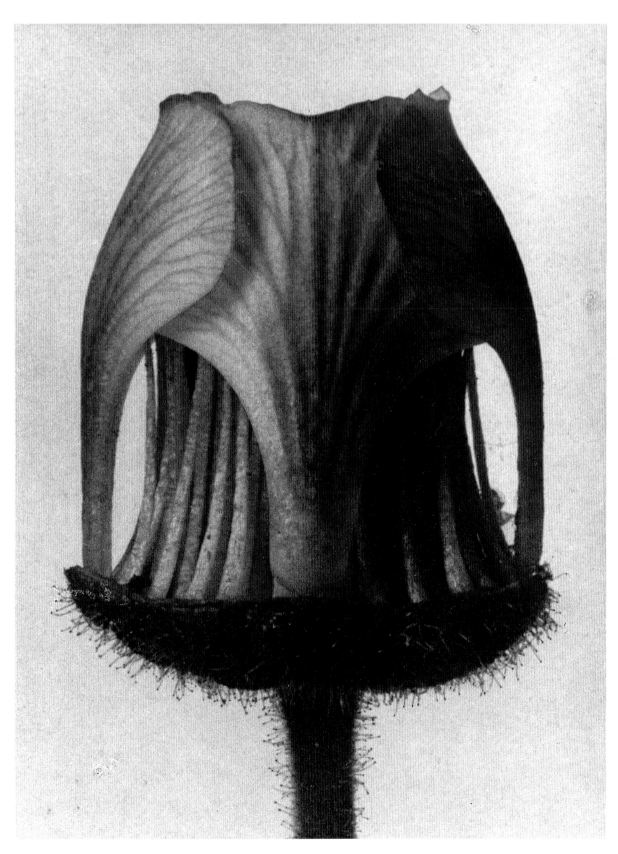

36 KARL BLOSSFELDT
Geum Rivale (Water Avens) 1900–25
Silver print

37 ERNST FUHRMANN

Tropaeolum Majus Mamm, Nasturtium Flowerbud c. 1923

Silver print

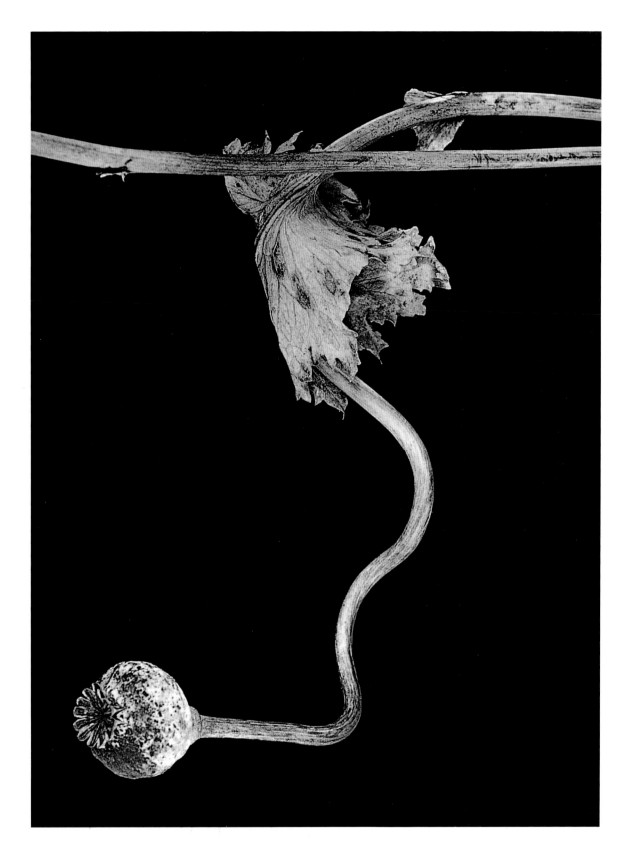

38 ERNST FUHRMANN
Seed Pod of a Poppy c. 1923
Silver print

39 HAROLD F. SHERWOOD
Bird of Paradise n.d.
Silver print from radiograph

40 DR ALBERT G. RICHARDS
Iris c. 1974–79
Silver print from radiograph

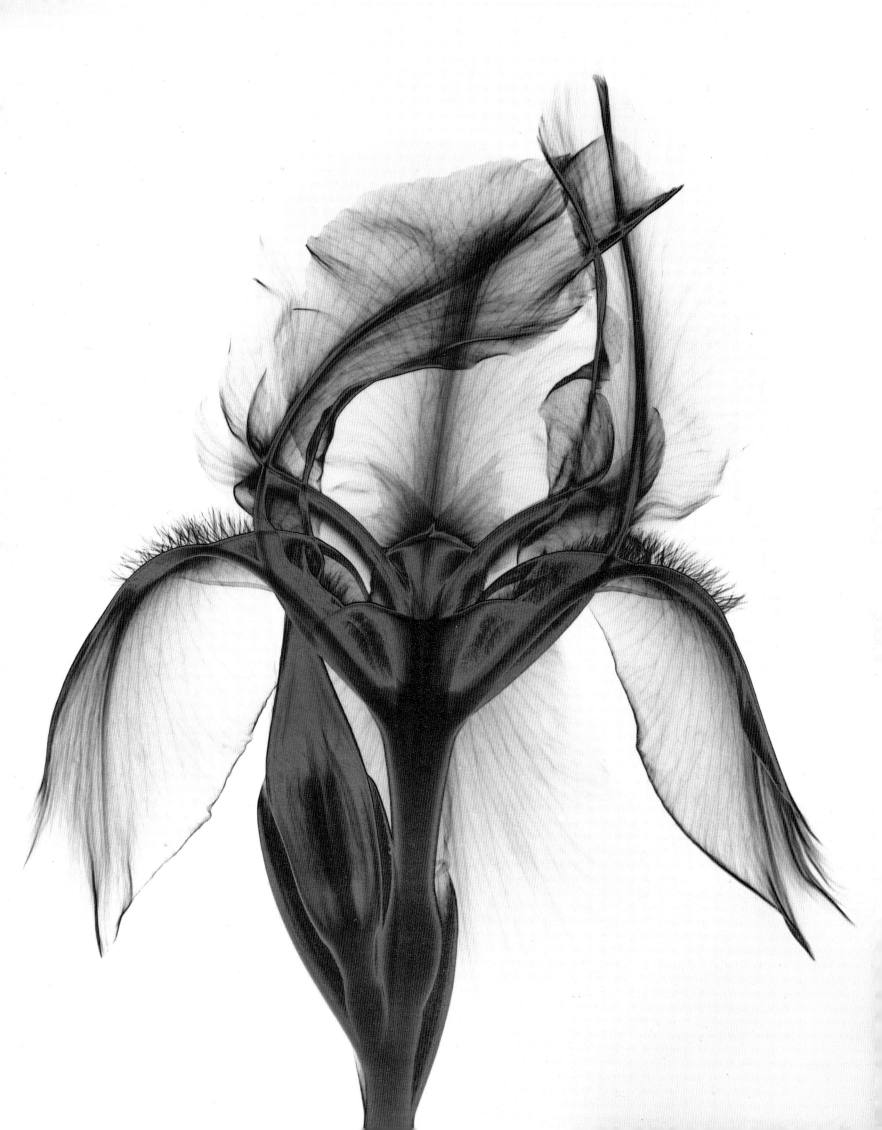

Persona

Duke For women are as roses, whose fair flower
        Being once displayed, doth fall that very hour.
Viola And so they are: alas, that they are so:
        To die, even when they to perfection grow.
        William Shakespeare, *Twelfth Night*

Since the Renaissance, flowers have been incorporated
in portraits to signify social status, professional interest or a specific
trait of personality and character. The appearance of a pink in a late Renaissance
portrait, for example, indicated that the sitter was married. Sometimes the significance was of a generalized nature: in most portraits of women, for instance, the
flower is an emblem of *femininity* rather than a signifier of a certain individuality. Flowers could stand for youth, beauty, virginity, innocence and vulnerability.

From the beginning photographic portraiture embraced these traditional associations, codified in the fashionable 'language of flowers'. As a result, men are
rarely depicted with flowers, unless judged atypically 'sensitive'- thus for example
we find the flower in a portrait of a Buddhist priest by Thérèse Le Prat, and in
portrayals of artists such as Salvador Dali by Jean Dieuzaide, Andy Warhol by
Dennis Hopper and Lucas Samaras by Arnold Newman.

Aside from its generalized emblematic function in portraits of women, the flower could also be employed with more specific symbolic intent. Fernand Khnopff,
for example, found in the arum lily both a graphic correspondence with the body
and a symbol of death which would have been instantly identifiable as such by
his late-19th-century viewers. And Robert Mapplethorpe found in the
orchid an ideal metaphor for his own rare and vulnerable talent.

41 FERNAND KHNOPFF
Arum Lily 1895
Photo by Alexandre, retouched, tinted and signed by Khnopff

42 HUGO ERFURTH
Young Woman with Hat c. 1902
Oil pigment print

43 AUGUST SANDER
Schwestern, Westerwald c. 1927
Silver print

44 HUGO ERFURTH
Otto Dix 1925
Gum print

45 JULIA MARGARET CAMERON
Mrs Duckworth, Freshwater 1874
Albumen print from wet collodion negative

46 THÉRÈSE LE PRAT
Buddhist Priest with Lotus, Angor, Indochina 1936
Silver print

47 CECIL BEATON
Marlene Dietrich 1932
Silver print

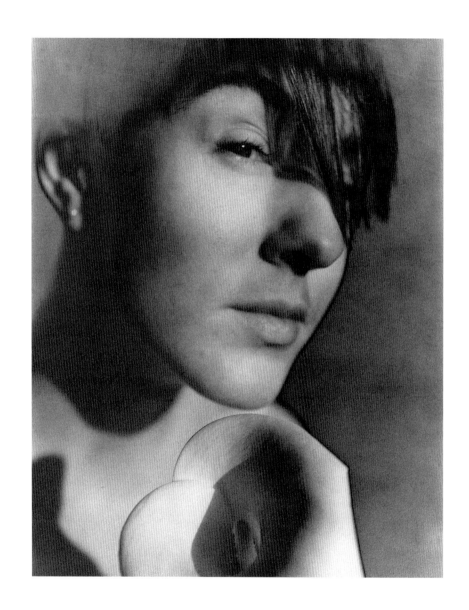

48 MICHAEL SPANO
With Lily 1986
Silver print

49 RAYMOND VOINQUEL
Foun Sen 1943
Silver print

50 ROBERT MAPPLETHORPE
Orchid with Hand 1983
Silver print

51 ANDRÉ KERTÉSZ
Chez Mondrian, Paris 1926
Silver print

52 HELEN LEVITT
New York 1942
Silver print

53 LOUIS FAURER
Eddie on Third Avenue & 54th Street, New York 1947
Silver print

54 EIKOH HOSOE
Yukio Mishima, from *Barakei,* 1961
Silver print

55 JEAN DIEUZAIDE
Dali in the Water 1953
Silver print

56 DENNIS HOPPER
Untitled (Andy Warhol) 1963
Silver print

57 ARNOLD NEWMAN
Lucas Samaras, New York 1980
Silver print

Essence

'The secret of a good photograph - which like a work of art may possess aesthetic qualities - is its realism . . . Let us therefore leave art to artists and endeavour to create photography which will last because of its photographic quality [which] hasn't been borrowed from another art.'

Albert Renger-Patzsch, 'Ziele', *Das Deutsche Lichtbild*, 1927

From the beginning photographers were driven to look deeper and more keenly at the world of nature than their forebears - whether artists or scientists - had been able to do. It was quickly recognized that the camera vastly extended human vision. Almost immediately photography was harnessed to the microscope, while lenses were tooled with ever greater precision, sources of artificial light refined and photographic chemistry developed. With the invention of the X-ray and the electron scan, we have been treated to a vision of a complex and ordered universe beyond our wildest imaginings.

Curiously, however, our astonishment is not easily sustained. The scientist in all of us may be satisfied, but the artist feels that some vital component, some key to a full understanding, has eluded us. And so we are more inclined to marvel at Man Ray's Rayograph than Harold Sherwood's radiograph. It dawns on us that true *essence* may be more than a ten-thousand-fold-magnification, or any other revelation that science alone can deliver.

Thus photographers probe and seek in their own ways, focusing in on a single petal or section of stem, as do Yasuhiro Ishimoto and Robert Mapplethorpe, or showing the plant whole and in its natural habitat, as does Edwin Hale Lincoln. Others, like Denis Brihat and Konrad Cramer, lean towards a painterly abstraction, while Imogen Cunningham crafts a clever balance between geometric abstraction and crystal-clear representation. And the dead or dying flower provides Cay Lang and Chris Enos with - ironically - a fresh beginning, as tired conventions of beauty are dismissed.

58 IMOGEN CUNNINGHAM
Amaryllis 1933
Silver print

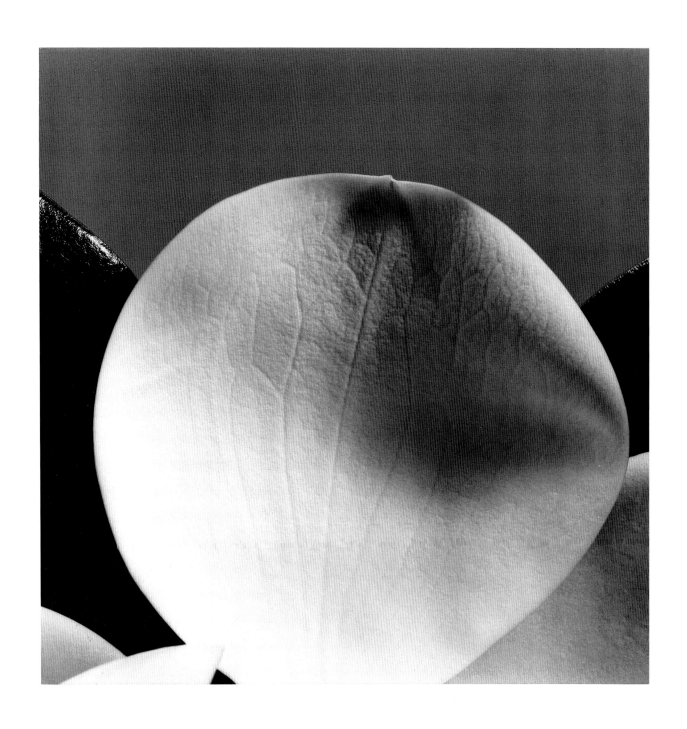

59 YASUHIRO ISHIMOTO
Southern Magnolia 1987
Silver print

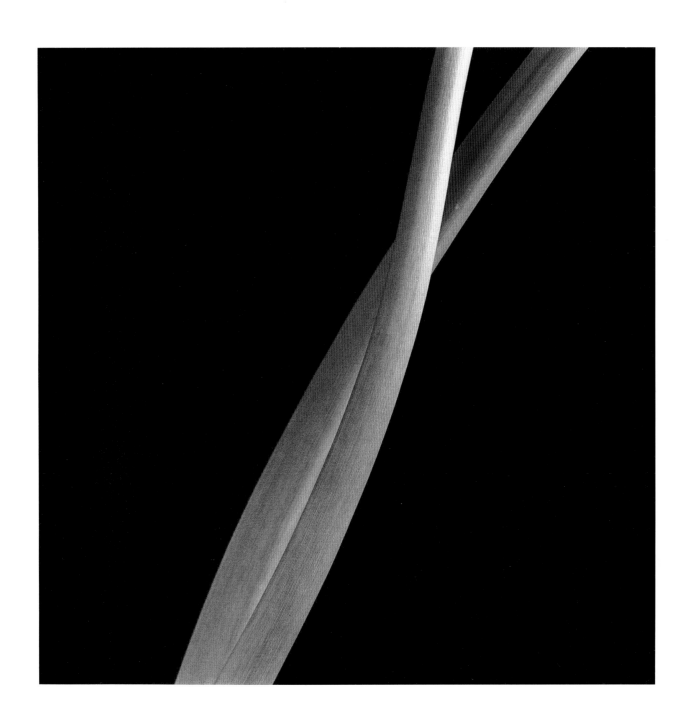

60 ROBERT MAPPLETHORPE
Stems 1985
Silver print

61 JOHN ATCHLEY
Untitled c. 1972
Polaroid print

62 YASUHIRO ISHIMOTO
Common Sunflower 1987
Silver print

63 DENIS BRIHAT
Black Tulip 1977
Selenium-toned silver print

64 KONRAD CRAMER
Rose Abstraction c. 1935
Silver print

65 JERRY UELSMANN
Untitled 1961
Silver print

66 SCOWEN & CO.
Angraecum Sesquipedale (Ceylon) *c.* 1870s
Albumen print

67 CAY LANG
Ophelia 1983
Ektacolour print

68 CHRIS ENOS
Poinsettia 1979
Polaroid 20 × 24 print

69 SCOWEN & CO.
Cattleya Trianae *c.* 1870s
Albumen print

70 EMMANUEL SOUGEZ
Untitled 1930
Silver print

71 ALMA LAVENSON
Chrysanthemum 1931
Silver print

72 CHARLES SHEELER
The Lily, Mount Kisco 1918—19
Silver print

73 EDWIN HALE LINCOLN
Nymphaea Advena, or Yellow Pond Lily,
Spatter-dock or Cow-Lily c. 1900−1910
Platinum print

74 EDWARD STEICHEN
Lotus, Mount Kisco 1915
Silver print

75 EMMANUEL SOUGEZ
Untitled 1930
Silver print

76 E. F. KITCHEN
Magnolia II 1986
Platinum/palladium print

77 IMOGEN CUNNINGHAM
Magnolia Blossom 1925
Silver print

78 ALINARI STUDIO
Ipomoea c. 1870s
Albumen print

Eros

'Roses at first were white
till they co'd not agree,
whether my Sappho's breast
or they more white sho'd be.'
Robert Herrick , 1591-1674

Since classical antiquity, if not earlier, flowers have
served as messengers of love - love of all types and degrees -
Platonic, motherly, filial, brotherly, marital, adulterous. Much of the flower rhetoric
in which the Victorians cloaked their speech was of love - love admitted, con-
summated, denied. Photography embraced these associations and extended
their reach; on the ubiquitous postcard, for example, the photograph stood in for
the flowers themselves as a kind of poor man's bouquet. Flowers were essential
elements of photographic keepsakes and mementos, especially when it came to
intimate portrayals of women, as we see in two early colour nudes by Charles
Adrien and Henri Bergon, where flowers, with their traditional associations of
innocence and purity, have perhaps been used to soften and disguise male lust.

The rose has always enjoyed special favour, its layers of petals corresponding
to layers of symbolism: erotic love in Classical times; the Virgin Mary's purity and
elevation; 'unwed status' in the Victorian's prim 'language of flowers'. But, as
ancient associations are obviously deeply engrained, we find the rose is chosen
as an emblem of prostitution by E.J. Bellocq, and as lascivious promise by Bert
Stern for his unabashed depiction of a modern Venus.

But the erotic is not the only dimension of love honoured by the photographers
present here. Flowers convey a message of self-adoration in George Platt Lynes's
parable; they speak of familial affection and joy for Sally Mann; and they signify
Platonic love and spiritual yearning for F. Holland Day
and Elisabeth Sunday.

79 ANONYMOUS PHOTOGRAPHER
Untitled c. 1910
Albumen print

80 ANONYMOUS PHOTOGRAPHER
Untitled c. 1920
Silver print

81 WILHELM VON GLOEDEN
Sicilian Youth 1890–1900
Albumen print

82 CHARLES ADRIEN
Untitled 1912
Autochrome plate

83 HENRI BERGON
Untitled c. 1910
Autochrome plate

84–86 ANONYMOUS PHOTOGRAPHER
Three French Postcards c. 1910

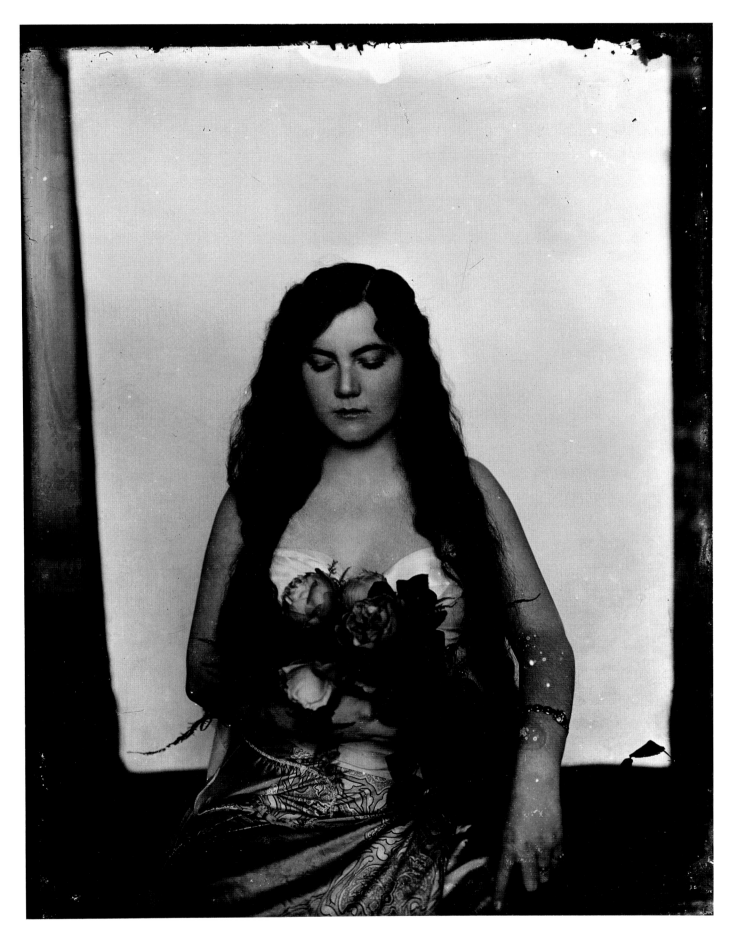

87 E. J. BELLOCQ
Untitled *c.* 1910
Modern print on printing-out paper by Lee Friedlander

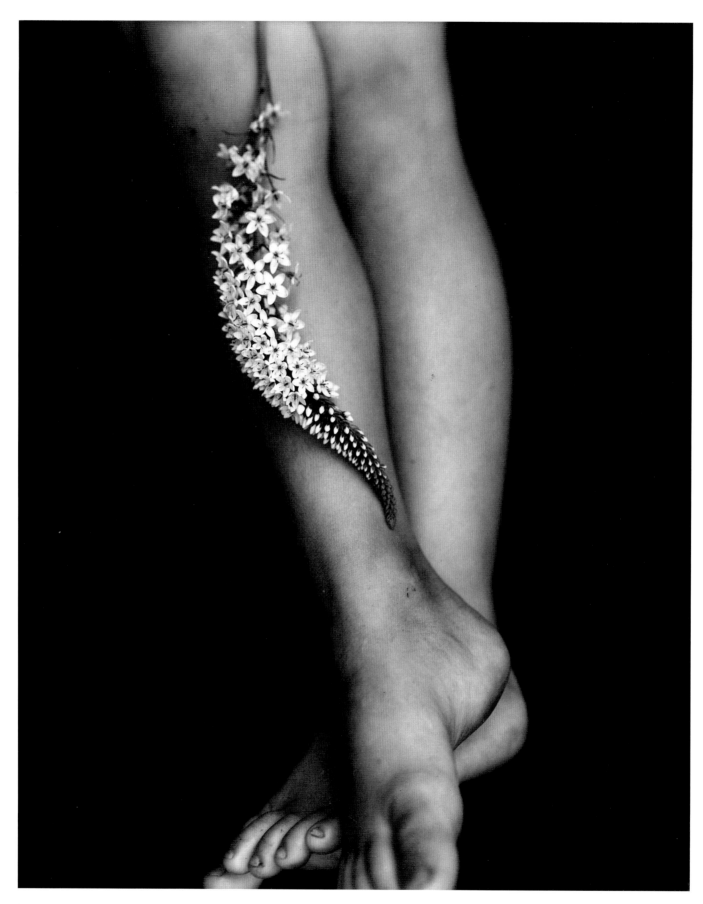

88 SALLY MANN
Gooseneck Loosestrife 1985
Silver print

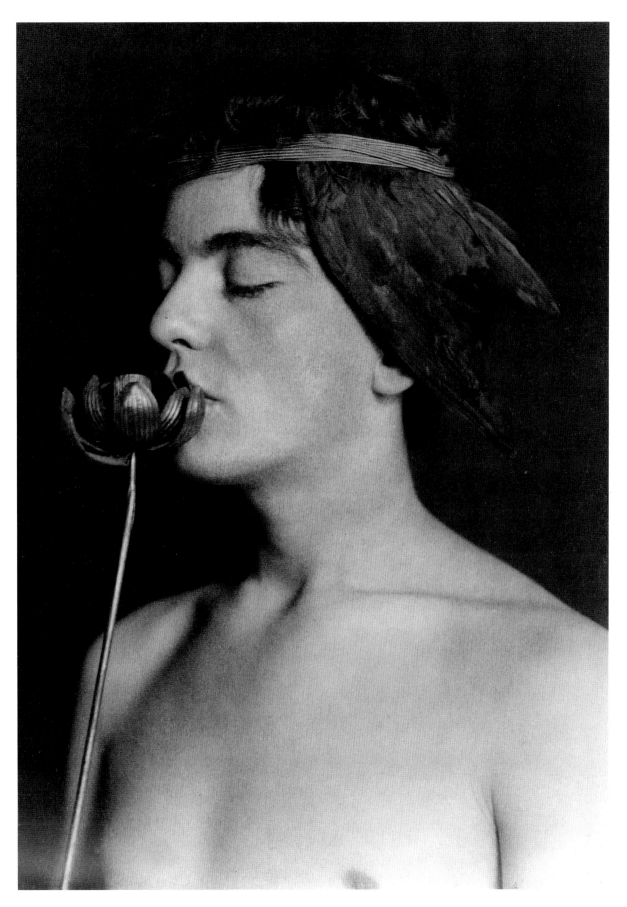

89 FREDERICK HOLLAND DAY
Hypnos c. 1896
Platinum print

90 FRANTIŠEK DRTIKOL
Nude c. 1930
Silver print

91 BERT STERN
Marilyn 1962
Silver print

92 WENDELL MACRAE
Nude c. 1938
Silver print

93 PAUL OUTERBRIDGE
Nude on Bed with Flowers c. 1936
Black and white silver print from original colour separation negative

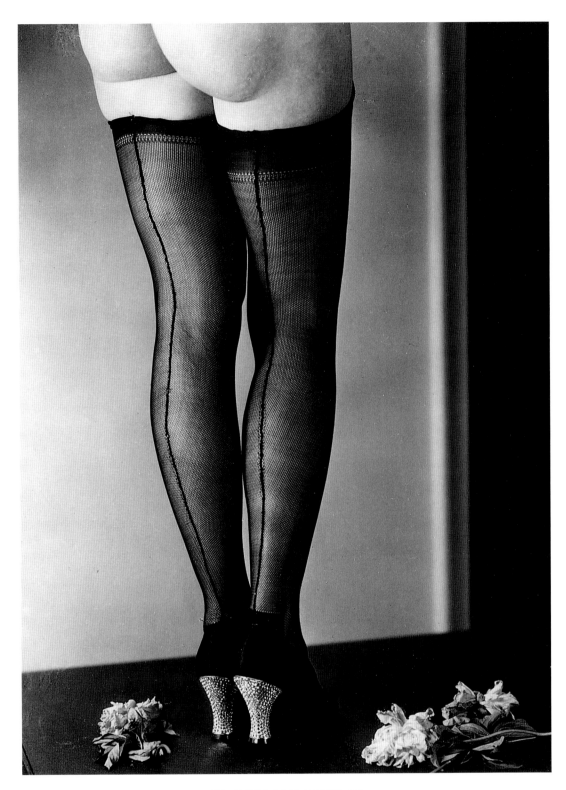

94 GEORGE PLATT LYNES
Untitled, from the series *Narcissus* 1937–39
Silver print

95 PAUL OUTERBRIDGE
Legs in Stockings with Flowers c. 1928
Silver print

96–98 ELISABETH SUNDAY
Floral Nude Triptych 1983
Toned silver prints

Hybrid

'The Old Masters have proved that the artist, once he has established his own idiom, once he has taken from nature the necessary means of expression, is free, legitimately free, to borrow his subjects from history, from the poets, from his own imagination.'

Odilon Redon, ` Le Salon de 1868', *La Gironde,* May 19, 1868

What the camera *sees* is not necessarily what the photographer *envisions,* and 'hybrid' imagery may be required to coax the latter into existence. Photographers have crafted a range of such hybridizing techniques, some of which - the painted photograph, for instance - are standard practice, while others, like Keiichi Tahara's etched transparency, are wholly original. Some hybrids have been engineered through manipulation of chemistry, as we see in a set of experimental works by Edward Steichen, through cameraless imagery of the kind Man Ray called Rayographs, and by means of light drawing during long time exposures - somewhat different approaches to which have been developed by Marvin Gasoi and David Lebe.

Collage and montage are venerable hybrids, allowing for startling juxtapositions and potent symbolic form; Gordon L. Bennett and Olivia Parker have adopted these formats for reflections on the passage of time and the relationship of nature and culture. Less traditional in format are the dismembered and reconstituted works by Lucas Samaras and the Starn twins, and the composite pictures built up from individual images by Stefan De Jaeger and Pierre Boogaerts, composites which resist, as the latter has put it, 'the comfort of frames'.

Less traditional, too, are the attempts of Suzanne Opton and Francis Bruguière to dissemble their subjects, to obstruct normal vision, in order to enhance *perception.*

99 ANONYMOUS PHOTOGRAPHER
Untitled c. 1910
Hand-coloured albumen print

100—103 EDWARD STEICHEN
Untitled c. 1940
Process-dye imbibition

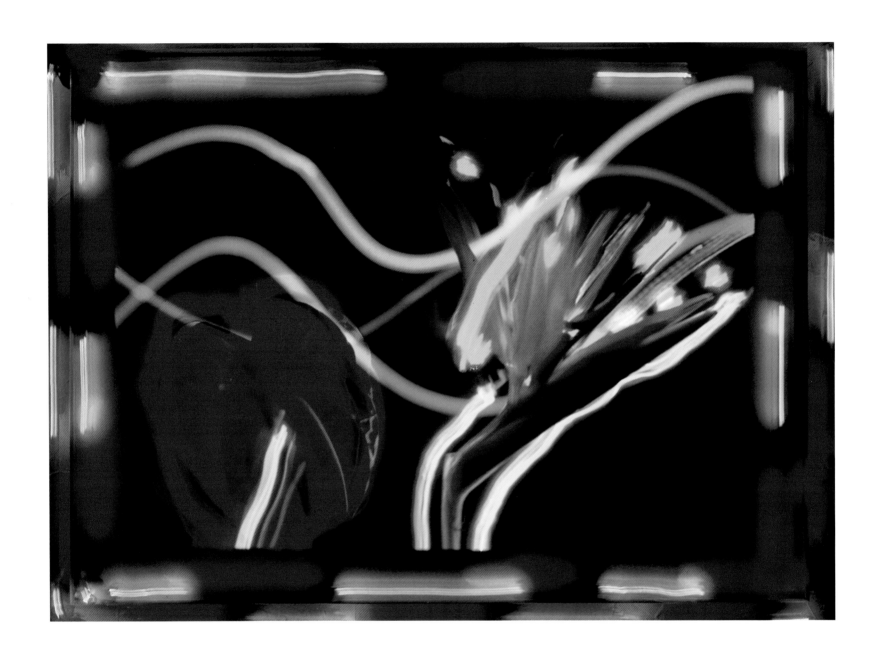

104 MARVIN GASOI
Bird of Paradise 1981
Cibachrome print

105 KEIICHI TAHARA
Untitled 1990
Fujichrome 50D with manipulated surface

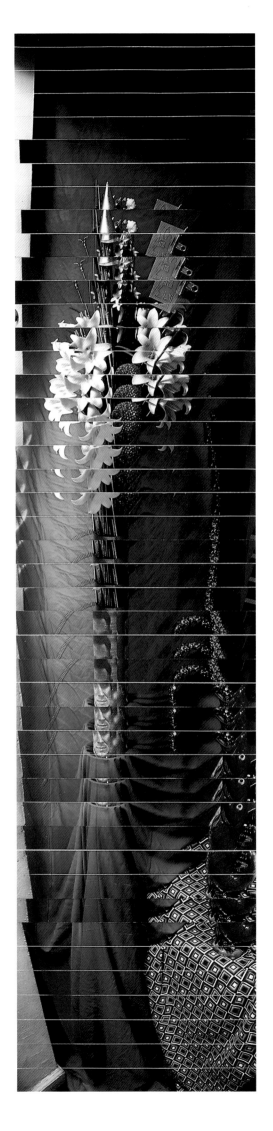

106 LUCAS SAMARAS
Lilies, Still Life 1983
Unique Polaroid Polacolour II assemblage

107 STARN TWINS
Rose 1982–88
Toned silver print with wood

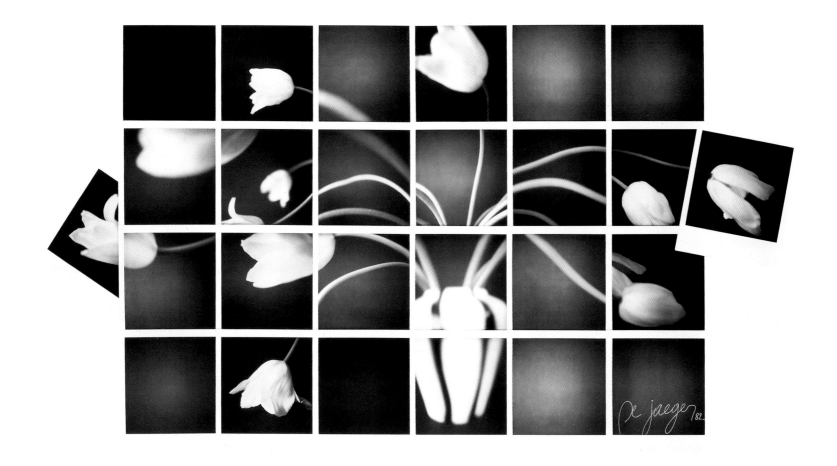

108 STEFAN DE JAEGER
Tulips for Sam 1982
Polaroid composite of twenty-six prints

109 DAVID LEBE
Scribble No. 23 1987
Silver print with watercolour

110 PIERRE BOOGAERTS
Thilandia 1986
Colour photograph

111 RICK HOCK
Natural History, Codex 1986
Manipulated Polaroid SX-70 composite of X-ray imagery
by A. G. Richards, etc. (See page 31)

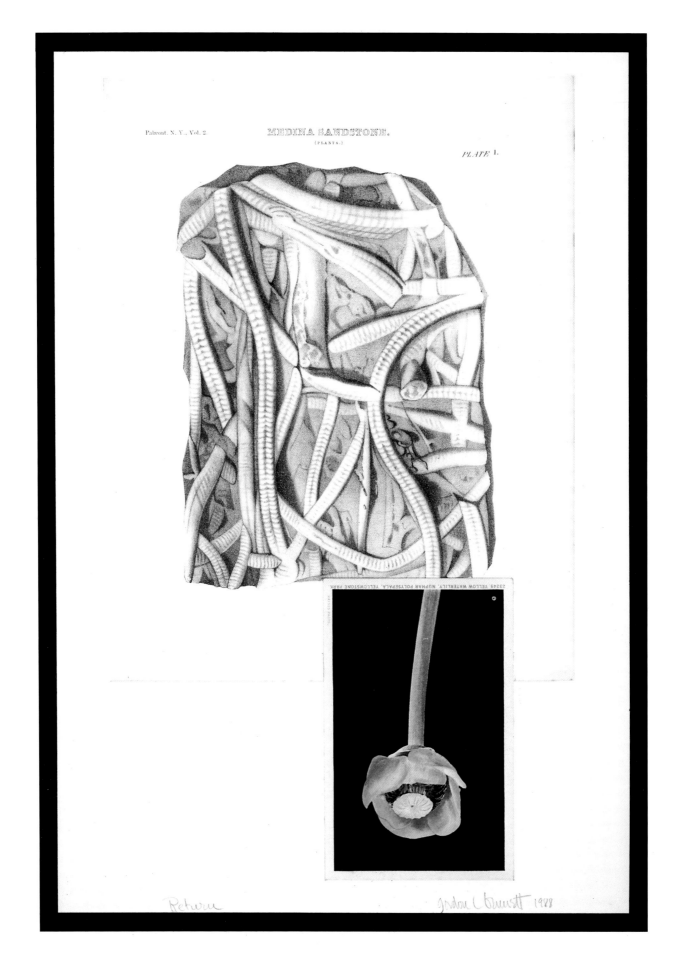

Paleont. N.Y., Vol. 2   MEDINA SANDSTONE.   PLATE I.
(PLANTS.)

112   GORDON L. BENNETT
Return 1988
Collage

113 OLIVIA PARKER
Blossoms 1982
Selenium-toned silver contact print

114 FRANCIS J. BRUGUIÈRE
Untitled c. 1936—40
Silver print by J. Enyeart from original negative

115 SUZANNE OPTON
Mock Gladiola 1983
Silver print

116 BARON ADOLF DE MEYER
Untitled 1928
Photogram, platinum print

117 MAN RAY
Rayograph 1922
Photogram, silver print

Anhang zu: Gerlach, Festons und decorative Gruppen.   Zieralphabete.   Verlag von Gerlach & Schenk in Wien.

I.

Déposé.

118 WALTER PETERHANS
Untitled c. 1926—36
Silver print

119 MARTIN GERLACH
page from *Festons und Decorative Gruppen
nebst einem Zieralphabete aus Pflanzen und Thieren
Jagd Touristen und anderen Geräthen,*
Vienna, Gerlach & Schenk 1893
Collotype, printed in colour

Arrangement

'We may arrange our flowers so that they form a beautiful bouquet consisting of all the colours of the rainbow, and so distribute the light that it appears to filter through the leafy meshes, and we feel sure in our hearts that they will make a perfect picture. But alas, how often are our hopes blighted, and disappointment is the reward we reap for our pains. And why? - because we photographers too often overlook the violent contrasts, and effects of light and shade, and we are too apt to forget that our photographs will not render the true gradations of tints and colours, in their respective values to the original.'

The Photographic News, July, 1888

Until the introduction of the Autochrome plate in the early 20th century, colour was not a viable option for the photographer challenged with the flower arrangement. As a consequence, early photographers were forced to concentrate their efforts on the depiction of form. So successfully was this achieved that many photographers today prefer the expressivity of black-and-white film over colour. 'I think it best', explains contemporary practitioner Yasuhiro Ishimoto, 'if people who see the photos tint the flowers with whatever colours come to their minds.'

Any observer with a keen eye will note how photographers have borrowed from the great Northern European tradition of flower painting; Charles Sheeler, for instance, has given us a quintessentially Modernist equivalent of an Ambrosius Bosschaert. Still other flower photographers have found oriental styles more to their liking. Whatever their inspiration, the finest photographic flower pieces add to the time honoured tradition some element which is purely photographic - De Meyer the play of light, the Alinari brothers pristine clarity, Steve Lovi a deliberate photographic/painterly ambiguity and Sheila Metzner an almost suffocating hothouse languor.

120 HEINRICH KÜHN
*Still Life c.*1920
Gum bichromate print

121 ALINARI STUDIO
Lilium Auratum (Goldband Lily) *c.* 1870s
Albumen print

122 BARON ADOLF DE MEYER
Waterlilies c. 1907
Platinum print

123 BARON ADOLF DE MEYER
Still Life c. 1907
Photogravure from *Camera Work*, No. 24, October 1908

124 CHARLES SHEELER
Zinnia and Nasturtium Leaves 1915
Silver print

125 JAN GROOVER
Untitled 1986
Contact silver print

126 MARTA HOEPFFNER
Composition with Shadows and Rose 1943
Silver print

127 ROBERT MAPPLETHORPE
Tulips 1987
Silver print

128 ANDRÉ KERTÉSZ
Melancholic Tulip, New York 1939
Silver print

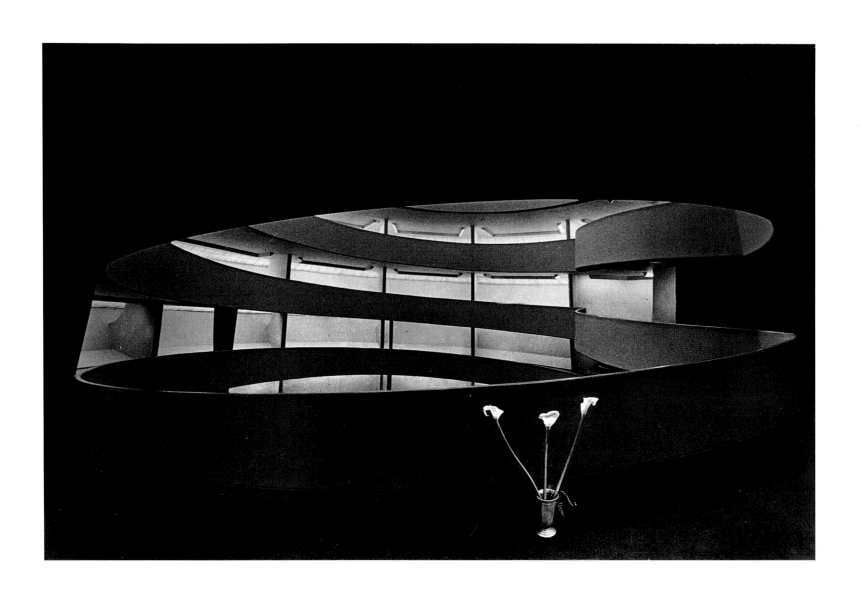

129 GÉRALD DUCIMETIÈRE
Some Flowers at the Solomon R. Guggenheim Museum c. 1980
Silver print

130 PAUL OUTERBRIDGE
Calla Lilies in a Vase 1926
Platinum print

131 ROSALIND MAINGOT
White Peonies 1958
Silver print

132 DON WORTH
Orchids and Caladiums, Mill Valley, California 1984
Ektachrome

133 SHEILA METZNER
Mondrian Orchid 1982
Fresson print

134 ROBERT MAPPLETHORPE
Tulips 1983
Toned photogravure

135 STEVE LOVI
Iceland Poppies 1988
Colour transparency

136 MORGAN WHITNEY
Still Life with Indian Lotus c. 1910
Platinum print

Mutation

'Now let the briar and the thistle flower
With violets; and the fair narcissus bloom
On junipers: let all things go awry,
And pines grow pears, since Daphnis is for death...'
Theocritus, *Idylls*, 3rd century BC

At its peak at mid-19th century, the 'language of flowers'
spoke mainly of love, youth and vitality, gaiety, innocence, perfection;
seldom did it allow for darker thoughts - Baudelaire's *fleurs du mal*. Nineteenth-century photographers wholeheartedly embraced this sentimental idealization. Floral greetings cards showed prettily arranged bouquets accompanied by a stanza of poetry or a biblical quotation. Photographers documented *fleurs ani-mées*, in which women and children (never men!) dressed up as flowers. They photographed visitors to fairgrounds posing happily as sunflowers, and domestic theatricals in which women worshipped monstrous mutations.

But in the 20th century certain photographers, and artists who have used photography as a means rather than an end, such as Gilbert & George, have found it difficult or impossible to embrace this maudlin sentimentality - which nonetheless still drives a thriving industry - preferring to employ the flower allegorically or metaphorically to reflect on graver and more substantial topics. The work of Tracey Holland investigates death and decay; the work of George Hugnet, perversity; the work of Gilbert & George, violent sexuality. John Stezaker and Victor Landweber look at our discordant relationship with nature; Joan Fontcuberta teasingly undermines our blind faith in science. Even when their sentiments are positive, and a sense of wonder and promise prevails, as in the work of Betty Hahn, Barbara Crane, Jerry Uelsmann and Doug Prince, the traditional language of
flowers is scrupulously avoided - or, in the case of
Brian Ogglesbee, savagely satirized.

137 HANS BELLMER
The Doll 1934–36
Silver print

138 ANONYMOUS PHOTOGRAPHER
Untitled n.d.
Tintype

139 ANONYMOUS PHOTOGRAPHER
Untitled n.d.
Tintype

140 JOAN FONTCUBERTA
Cala Rasca, from *Herbarium* 1983
Silver print

141 JOAN FONTCUBERTA
Giliandria Escoliforcia, from *Herbarium* 1984
Silver print

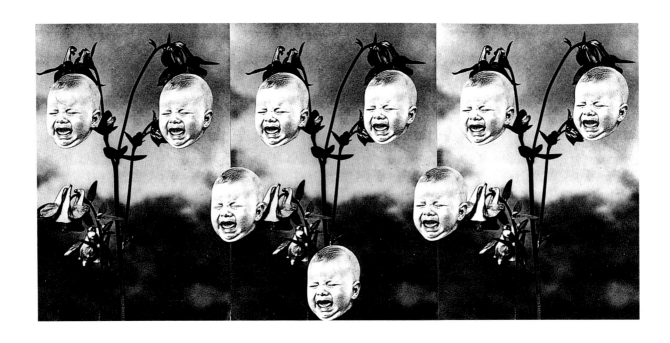

142 JOHN STEZAKER
from *The Underworld Series* 1984
Photocollage

143 OLIVIA PARKER
Stairway 1987
Polacolour print

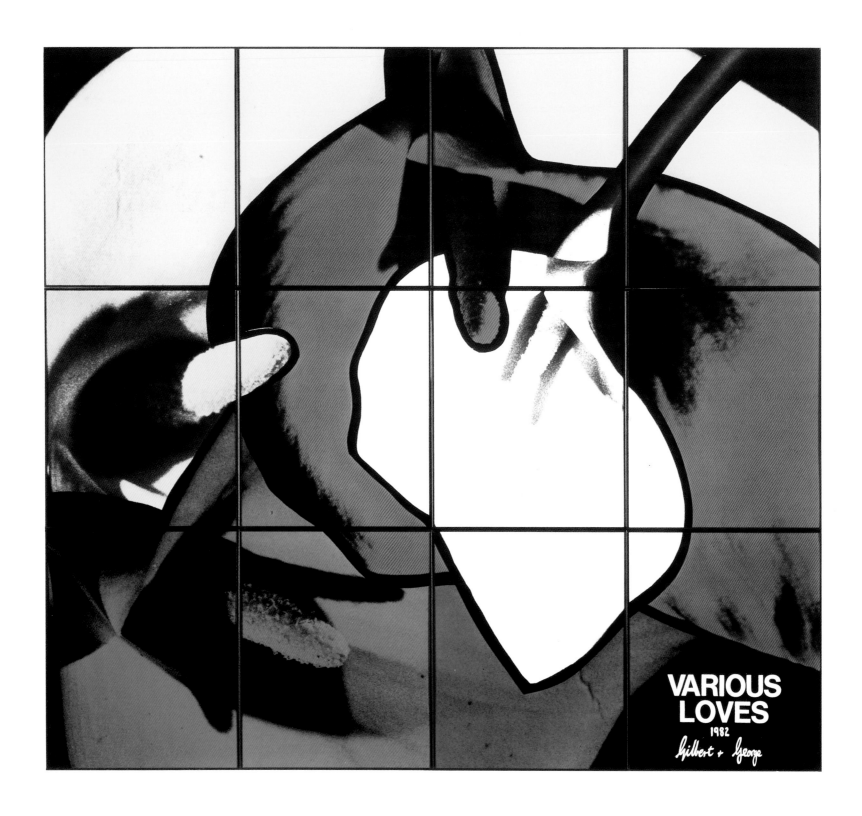

144 GILBERT & GEORGE
Various Loves 1982
No medium provided

145 GEORGE HUGNET
Preliminary Initiation into the Secrets of the Forest 1936
Photocollage

146 BETTY HAHN
Iris with Watercolour 1985
Cyanotype with watercolour

147 BARBARA CRANE
from *Visions of Enarc* 1983—88
Polaroid 20 × 24 print

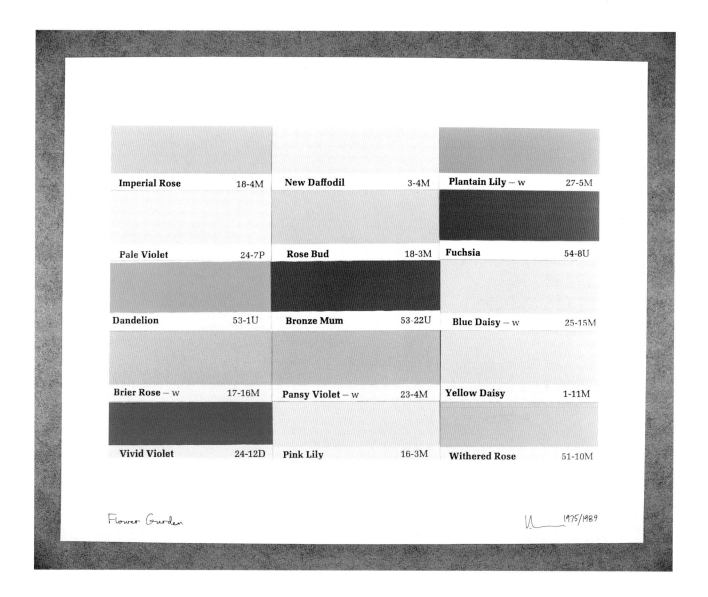

Imperial Rose 18-4M	**New Daffodil** 3-4M	**Plantain Lily** — w 27-5M
Pale Violet 24-7P	**Rose Bud** 18-3M	**Fuchsia** 54-8U
Dandelion 53-1U	**Bronze Mum** 53-22U	**Blue Daisy** — w 25-15M
Brier Rose — w 17-16M	**Pansy Violet** — w 23-4M	**Yellow Daisy** 1-11M
Vivid Violet 24-12D	**Pink Lily** 16-3M	**Withered Rose** 51-10M

Flower Garden 1975/1989

148 BRIAN OGGLESBEE
Arrangement 1986
Colour coupler print

149 VICTOR LANDWEBER
Flower Garden 1975/1989
Colour coupler print (Duraflex)

150 TRACEY HOLLAND
Incubus I 1989
Cibachrome print

151 RUTH THORNE-THOMSEN
Flora Bella 1986
Contact silver print

152 VILEM KRIZ
from *Seance, Berkeley* 1977
Silver print

153 DOUG PRINCE
Transfigurations No. 9 1989
Silver print from combined negatives

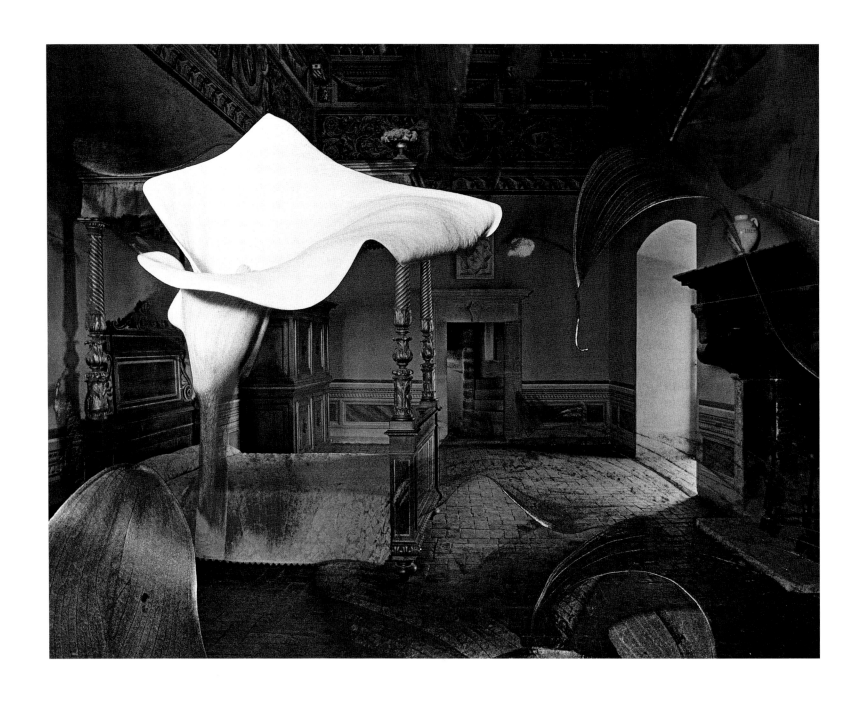

154 DOUG PRINCE
Italian Observations No. 4 1984
Silver print from combined negatives

155 JERRY UELSMANN
Untitled 1968
Silver print

156–59 DUANE MICHALS
A Dream of Flowers 1986
Silver prints

Observation

'The man who lives in his eyes is continually confronted with scenes and spectacles that compel with attention or admiration and demand an adequate reaction. To pass on without pause is impossible . . . Photography, to many of its addicts, is a convenient and simple means of discharging these ever recurring debts to the visual world.'

Edwin Smith, 1973

It is a rare photographer whose eye has not been drawn to a flower on some occasion, whatever his general disposition towards nature. Some, however, have nurtured a special affection for the flower in its natural habitat, free of man's decorative urges. Edwin Smith, to give one example, fashioned images of his native British flora of which Ruskin would have been proud. In France, Denis Brihat looked upon the blossoming countryside with similar feeling. Parks and gardens have also attracted photographers: Eugène Atget seems to have preferred flowers in the most informal of these settings, rather than subordinated to the grand design of Versailles or St Cloud. Stephen Shore found in Monet's gardens at Giverny a daunting challenge, and rose to the occasion with a series of superb colour studies. Lee Friedlander, on the other hand, preferred the springtime flowers of Japan, returning on numerous occasions to record them.

For many other photographers, however, it is the *un*natural flower which exerts the strongest attraction: street photographers like Robert Walker, working the rich vein of colour, or Jerome Liebling, Louis Faurer and Ken Josephson are struck by revealing juxtapositions of flowers - real and otherwise - which they find at every turn in the urban jungle. Apparently, they seem to say, human beings cannot live without the solace of flowers, especially - and here Edward Weston and Josef Sudek offer evidence - in matters of death.

160 EUGÈNE ATGET
Oriental Poppy c. 1910–20
Albumen print

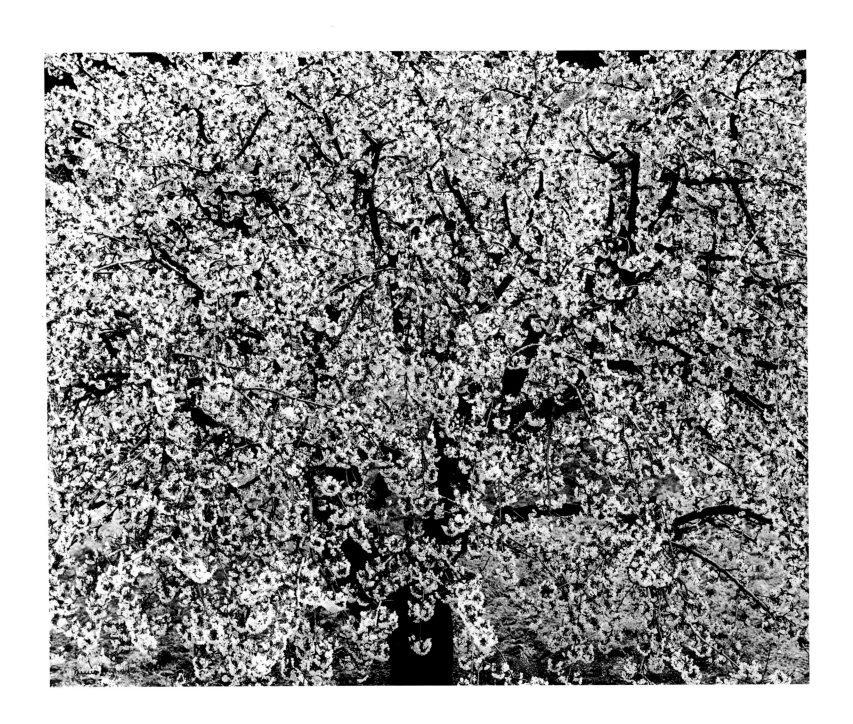

161 DENIS BRIHAT
Cherry Tree 1984
Silver print with bleach manipulation

162 STEPHEN SHORE
Giverny, France 1982
Type C colour print

163 ROBERT WALKER
Montreal 1987
Cibachrome print

164 JEROME LIEBLING
Communion Dress, Malaga, Spain 1966
Silver print

165 ALBERT RENGER-PATZSCH
Hyacinth c. 1925—30
Silver print

166 LOUIS FAURER
Market Street, Philadelphia c. 1944
Silver print

167 KENNETH JOSEPHSON
Chicago 1961
Silver print

168 IZIS
Windowsill, Paris before 1953
Silver print

169 EDWARD WESTON
Willie 1941
Silver print

170 JOSEF SUDEK
Walk in the Cemetery of Mala Strana 1946
Silver print

171 LEE FRIEDLANDER
Kyoto 1977
Silver print

172 EDWIN SMITH
Westmorland near Levens Hall, Beech and Garlic 1962
Silver print

Quintessence

'It is a flower - if you like. But the fact is, I do not like. What makes you think the arum is a flower? Not a petal, not a sepal in sight. The green of its stem widens out with neither suture nor joint, flares into a cornet, and then whitens. The white convolvulus draped over the hedges knows better, the long pendant of the datura is a poisonous jewel. But you like the arum, its minimum of refinement, its stiffness; "What lovely simplicity, what strength," you say . . . Am I trying to pick a quarrel with you or with the arum?'

Colette, 'Calf's-foot arum', *Pour un Herbier*, 1948

The arum or calla lily is the aristocrat of
flowers, to which, admits Colette grudgingly, the bouquets of the
West give pride of place. Of all flowers (even winning out over the beloved sunflower) it is the favourite of photographers, just as the chrysanthemum was the favourite of the Impressionists and the crown imperial that of the Dutch masters. The calla is a black-tie flower; the quintessentially *photographic* flower; its form, line and texture transcribe beautifully into the language of black-and-white photography. Thus it presents itself to Man Ray's lens, sleek, handsome and confident (and enhanced by an elegant penumbra), then takes a deep bow for Robert Mapplethorpe, modestly acknowledging its undisputed preeminence.

For Imogen Cunningham (in one of many images) it is well suited to profile; in the hands of Carlotta Corpron it performs a rhythmic cascade; in Dain Tasker's X-ray its cornet is transformed into a swirling, diaphanous veil, as insubstantial as smoke. Even in its dissolution the arum lily is magnificent; Chris Enos's camera reveals the richest of ecclesiastical garments, all velvet and gold, while Barbara
Norfleet catches it in its private agony, ravished by time,
yet still unbowed.

173 MAN RAY
Calla Lilies 1930
Silver print, solarized

174 IMOGEN CUNNINGHAM
Single Calla c. 1929
Silver print

175 ROBERT MAPPLETHORPE
Calla Lily with Shadow 1986
Silver print

176 WILLIAM GILES
Calla Lily, Oregon 1975
Silver print

177 ANSEL ADAMS
Untitled 1931
Silver bromide print

178 CARLOTTA CORPRON
Calla Lilies 1948
Silver print, solarized

179 ROBERT MAPPLETHORPE
Calla Lily 1988
Toned photogravure

180 DR DAIN TASKER
Lily — An X-ray 1930
Toned silver print from radiograph

181 CHRIS ENOS
Calla Lily 1979
Polaroid 20 × 24 print

182 BARBARA NORFLEET
Untitled 1981
Cibachrome print

183 EDWARD WESTON
Lily and Rubbish 1939
Silver print

1 Tony Boussenot (French, 1860s). The purpose of this artful arrangement (if there is one other than the sheer pleasure of its execution) cannot be ascertained, as little is known of the photographer or his work. It is a plate (No. 28) from an album entitled *Les Fleurs*; most likely the images were meant, as with those of a number of commercial photographers, as models for painters or students. The oval mount suggests that the image was not primarily conceived as a *picture*, as all the visual interest is concentrated in the flower arrangement itself. Courtesy The J. Paul Getty Museum, Malibu, California.

2 Anonymous (French, active 1870s). The heavy draperies which all but overpower the two floral arrangements are unmistakably French, of the kind we associate with academic painting of the second Empire. Everything in this picture is meticulously arranged: the tassels of the fabric offset the upward thrust of the blooms; one arrangement has been placed against a dark background, the other against a light one; the containers are of very different shapes and textures. All this would suggest that the picture was made as a model for students of the fine arts. Courtesy National Gallery of Canada, Ottawa.

3 Roger Fenton (British, 1819–1869). The photographer's flower and fruit studies, of which there were some 40, are indebted to the Dutch flower piece for their basic structure, but what Fenton makes of his subject matter photographically is all his own. By the time he turned to these studies, Fenton had a distinguished body of work behind him: landscapes and architectural subjects, cityscapes, photographs of the Crimean War and portraits. Here he has chosen to focus on the world writ small. Shortly after the series was complete, Fenton gave up photography. Courtesy The Royal Photographic Society, Bath.

4 Adolphe Braun (French, 1811–1877). Braun's early and impressive contribution to flower photography, dating from 1853 and possibly earlier, owes something to the example of the Dutch still life, but only insofar as his more formal radial compositions were concerned. When it came to more random arrangements, he was less inhibited. Indeed, one writer in the textile industry judged Braun's models to be superior to the conventional lithographs after Van Spaendonck which had been used by traditional designers. Courtesy Gordon L. Bennett Collection, Kentfield, California.

5 Eugène Chauvigné (French, dates unknown). Very little is known of the photographer. Like Braun, he may have been in the business of selling his studies to designers and artists for use as source material or reference works. His oval surrounds and roughly cropped prints suggest that his interest was specifically directed to the flower or flowers – that is, not to the creation of a pleasing 'picture'. *See also 7.* Courtesy Bibliothèque Nationale, Paris.

6 Charles Aubry (French, 1811–1877). Aubry did his best to market his flower photographs to schools of industrial design, with limited success. Today, however, they are considered by many collectors and curators to be among the finest flower studies of the 19th century. Courtesy Bibliothèque Nationale, Paris.

7 Eugène Chauvigné (French, dates unknown). *See also 5.* Courtesy Bibliothèque Nationale, Paris.

8 Hippolyte Bayard (French, 1801–1887). Bayard's picture of an informal arrangement of summer flowers is one of the earliest flower pieces in photography. Talbot had made some earlier, but none which compare aesthetically. Bayard apparently loved his garden, made studies of its implements, and took his own portrait there. The placement of the vase on the table, the clues as to receding space in the tablecloth, show an easy familiarity with Dutch flower pieces, such as those of Jan Davidsz de Heem. Courtesy Museum Folkwang, Essen.

9 Frederick Hollyer (British, 1837–1933). Hollyer's image may remind the viewer of musical notes in a score. In any event, the strong vertical lines of the wall act as an anchoring device for the riot of petals and stamens, which cascade diagonally across them. Courtesy The J. Paul Getty Museum, Malibu, California.

10 Reverend D. T. K. Drummond (British, 1806–1888). Courtesy Gordon L. Bennett Collection, Kentfield, California.

11 Edward Steichen (American, 1879–1973). *See also 14, 15, 74, 100–103; p. 19.* Courtesy Hallmark Photographic Collection, Hallmark Cards, Inc., Kansas City, Missouri.

12 Anonymous (French?, active 1840s). The daguerreotype seems to have been rarely used for still-life studies, perhaps because flower paintings, watercolours and engravings had reached such a state of perfection that the monochromatic medium of photography was deemed insufficient. This example comes from the collection of Gabriel Cromer (1873–1934), one of the earliest collectors of photographs, cameras and photographic ephemera. Courtesy International Museum of Photography at George Eastman House, Rochester, New York.

13 Auguste Lumière (French, 1862–1954); **Louis Lumière** (French, 1864–1948). This luminous stereo Autochrome was produced in 1907, the year the Lumière Brothers introduced their Autochrome plate, having taken some four years to make it practical. The company Lumière & Sons had been formed by their father in Lyons in 1882 for the manufacture of photographic dry plates. The brothers had been involved in colour research since at least 1892. The choice of a flower arrangement for this example was probably made to show off the new medium's colour capabilities, and the stereo effect would have heightened this new experience. Courtesy The J. Paul Getty Museum, Malibu, California.

14 Edward Steichen (American, 1879–1973). This print is the end result of an extensive experimental printing of one negative using a method known as process-dye imbibition. The meticulous search for the most expressive result was characteristic of Steichen's approach both to photography and to flower cultivation. He took great pride in his own hybrid delphiniums, arranging an exhibition of them at the Museum of Modern Art in 1936 (see p. 19). *See also 11, 15, 74, 100–103.* Courtesy International Museum of Photography at George Eastman House, Rochester, New York.

15 Edward Steichen (American, 1879–1973). *See also 11, 14, 74, 100–103; p. 19.* Courtesy International Museum of Photography at George Eastman House, Rochester, New York.

16 Heinrich Kühn (Austrian, 1866–1944). Kühn was a leading member of the Pictorialist movement and a member of the eminent society The Linked Ring. From 1896 he was one of the chief exponents of the gumbichromate method, but he was also well versed in other techniques, such as the oil transfer shown here and Autochrome. Deeply interested in colour, he produced prints in rich blues, greens, reds and browns, and, on occasion, in full colour. This casual arrangement of phlox in a simple jug in front of a window is typical of the kind of quiet, domestic scene he loved to depict and at which he excelled. *See also 120.* Courtesy National Gallery of Canada, Ottawa.

17 Anonymous (American, active 1930s/1940s). The flowering plant shown here is a model which presumably has just been completed for the Field Museum. Although obviously made as a document, several aspects of the photograph make for unintended humour: the professional detachment of the observer, the theatrical 'gesture' of the plant itself, like a star performer submitting to a television interview; the plant seems to be standing, so to speak, its own ground, which enhances the anthropomorphic effect. The admiring botanist is Paul C. Standley, a prolific author and botanical expert known for his phenomenal memory. He could identify at sight the majority of the more than 20,000 species of Mexico and Central America. Courtesy Field Museum of Natural History, Chicago (Negative #78580).

18, 19 Scowen & Co. (Ceylon, active 1870s to 1890s). The English conquered Ceylon in 1796. Firms such as Scowen & Co., founded around 1876, produced records for commerce and industry of the various plantation economies, the railroads, municipal buildings, etc., and city views, native types and ancient ruins for the tourist market. Such care went into Scowen & Co.'s flower studies, however, that it seems evident that tourists alone were not the intended buyers; Europe's horticulturalists would have provided a far more lucrative market. The firm's activities do not seem to have continued beyond the late 1890s. *See also 66, 69.* Courtesy Gordon L. Bennett Collection, Kentfield, California.

20 Dr Hans Shafer (German?, active 1930s). Courtesy Field Museum of Natural History, Chicago (Negative #37003).

21 Edward Thomson Harper (American, 1857–1921). A complete plant has been laid out in the manner of the botanical specimen and photographed with clarity. As a record of a living plant, the photograph has a decided advantage for the botanist over its alternative, the dried specimen. Courtesy Field Museum of Natural History, Chicago (Negative #20038).

22 Henry Troth (American, 1863–1948). Troth's naturalistic photograph of a pitcher plant allows for close study of a complete plant without any distracting background detail. It also enables the viewer to consider various stages of florescence, from the emerging bud to the open bloom. Such sensitive portrayals – plant portraits, as botanists call them – allowed Troth's work to be included in books of poetry as well as botany. Courtesy International Museum of Photography at George Eastman House, Rochester, New York.

23 Anonymous (active 1930s/1940s). Courtesy Field Museum of Natural History, Chicago (Negative #80042).
24 William Henry Fox Talbot (British, 1800–1877). This is quite possibly the first photograph of a flower ever made: at the very least it is among the earliest. Talbot began his experiments in the form of photogenic drawings in 1834 and by 1835 had established several ways of permanently fixing the image. Cut rather carelessly from a piece of paper, this image is typical of his earliest efforts. In his notes from 1835 we find the following: 'Paper washed with salt and silver [of a certain strength] and darkened in sunshine: the figure of a plant, etc., remaining white.' Further evidence for a date of 1835 is the fact that the image is a negative; as Gail Buckland points out: 'Up to 1835 all the photogenic drawings were negative, in other words, had their highlights and shadows reversed' (*Fox Talbot and the Invention of Photography*, London, 1980, p. 29).

There is a possibility, however, that the image may have been made in 1839, as it appears to have been fixed in hypo, which Talbot did not adopt until then. On the other hand, he may have taken the image earlier and had it rewashed and fixed at a later date. This would seem to be the case, judging from remarks addressed to the Royal Society in 1839, in which he outlined the control he had by then achieved, by contrast with which our example seems crude indeed: 'For example, nothing can be more perfect than the image [that is, his process at this time] gives of leaves and flowers, especially with a summer sun; the light passing through the leaves *delineates every ramification of their nerves*' (author's italics). In any event, we have Talbot's own word that he had been making studies since 1834. Courtesy National Gallery of Canada, Ottawa.
25, 26 Anna Atkins (British, 1797–1871); **Ann Dixon** (British, 1799–1864). Atkins's father, John George Children, was an eminent scientist, and as Secretary of the Royal Society was present when Talbot presented his paper *Some Account of the Art of Photogenic Drawing* on 21 February 1839. Soon after, and again the following year, Talbot sent Children samples of his photography to his home. Children shared these experiences with his daughter and encouraged her own scientific endeavours. The Children family was also close to the Herschel family, and on frequent visits Atkins had ample opportunity to learn the simple process of cyanotype which Sir John Herschel had invented in 1842. Atkins adopted the method for her own work, the documentation of British algae, which was published in parts between 1843 and 1853, after which she turned to ferns and flowering plants.

Ann Dixon was a close friend who had joined Atkins after the trauma of Children's death in 1852. Dixon was to prove a great help in the continuation of Atkins's work, with which she was already familiar, having collected plants with her for a number of years.

The examples shown here were made with specimens sent from North America. Courtesy (Top) The J. Paul Getty Museum, Malibu, California; (Bottom) Fraenkel Gallery, San Francisco, California.
27 Louis Ducos du Hauron (French, 1837–1920). Ducos du Hauron was a pioneering scientist in the area of colour photography. Having made substantial strides towards a system which would allow one-shot colour photography, he published in 1869 *Les Couleurs en photographie*, a treatise which provided a sound theoretical basis for future investigators. He also achieved positive results from his *Trichromie* method, a carbon process which eventually evolved into modern assembly printing. At the time, however, the method was not practical. True colour photography would have to await the invention of the Autochrome plate by the

Lumière brothers in 1907. Nevertheless, this contact print of leaves and flowers is a magnificent accomplishment, the first known photograph of flowers in colour (discounting of course the hand-coloured variety). Ducos du Hauron's work was much admired in the 19th century, and was regularly exhibited in Paris. In 1900 he received a medal for his efforts from the Royal Photographic Society in London. Courtesy Société Française de Photographie, Paris.
28–31 Pietro Guidi (Italian, active 1870s). Little is known of Guidi, other than that he lived and worked as a photographer around San Remo, photographing landscape and architecture along with the kinds of botanical documents shown here. These latter are highly accomplished works in the tradition of such master botanical illustrators as the 18th-century Georg Ehret. Courtesy Lee Gallery, Boston.
32 E. Reynaud (French, dates unknown). Reynaud's photographic studies may be the first such works to be produced in the service of botany. Courtesy Bibliothèque Nationale, Paris.
33 William James Stillman (American, 1828–1901). Stillman was a pre-Raphaelite painter and photographer, and a friend and devotee of John Ruskin. Courtesy Schaffer Library, Union College, Schenectady, New York.
34–36 Karl Blossfeldt (German, 1865–1932). Initially Blossfeldt was interested in making photographs which would provide textile designers, ironworkers and art students with reference material, much as Braun and Aubry had done in the 19th century (*See 4, 6*). However, his interest soon transcended these narrow parameters as he began to develop his thesis that artistic form had been derived from nature. To prove this he made thousands of enlargements of plant forms which exposed structures, patterns and rhythms not visible to the naked eye, putting his case forcefully before the public in two splendid books, *Urform der Kunst* (Archetypes of Art), 1928, and *Wundergarten der Natur* (Wondergarden of Nature), 1932. Courtesy © Karl Blossfeldt Archive, Ann and Jürgen Wilde, Zülpich, Germany.
37, 38 Ernst Fuhrmann (German, 1886–1956). It is sometimes said of Fuhrmann that he was not the author of his pictures, but this is misleading. It is true that he commissioned other photographers to take pictures, but there is little doubt that they did so according to his specifications and, moreover, an unknown quantity were certainly made by him. Courtesy Kicken/Pauseback Gallery, Cologne.
39 Harold F. Sherwood (American, b. 1908). Sherwood was a research specialist in the field of low-voltage radiography with the Eastman Kodak Company in Rochester, New York, and the author of several articles in professional journals. Courtesy Hunt Institute for Botanical Documentation, Carnegie-Mellon University, Pittsburgh, Pennsylvania.
40 Dr Albert G. Richards (American, b. 1917). Dr Richards began his hobby of thirty years on a whim, when he X-rayed a daffodil at the University of Michigan where he was teaching radiography to dental students. His collection now contains some 3,700 floral radiographs. Richards had no professional background in botany but has always been an avid gardener. Recently he has begun to radiograph the flowers of trees and to make three-dimensional radiographs. Courtesy The J. Paul Getty Museum, Malibu, California.
41 Fernand Khnopff (Belgian, 1858–1921). Khnopff is considered by many to be the most important of the Belgian Symbolist painters. In his youth he was influenced by his reading of Flaubert, Baudelaire and the Parnassian poet Leconte de Lisle. He professed to disdain photography as merely 'an agreeable pastime for an idler', but practiced it secretly – so secretly that his closest

friends discovered the fact only after his death. Realism, however, he believed should be held at arm's length, and the picture-making kept entirely under the control of the maker: '...he can do what he likes with it, and modify any part of it as he pleases, up to the very last moment'. In this particular image, he seems to have had another photographer make the image, probably to his specification, and he has then retouched, tinted and signed it. This act of commissioning should not be seen as casting doubt on the work's authenticity; as Edward Lucie-Smith points out, Khnopff 'had the dandy's fanatical interest in precision. However strange his compositions, they are never accidental. Every effect is calculated, every detail precisely and deliberately placed' (*Symbolist Art*, London, 1972, p. 122). There is a fascinating correspondence between the contours of the woman's body, particularly her arm, and the structure of the plant. Courtesy © Copyright Bibliothèque Royale Albert Ie, Cabinet des Estampes, Brussels.
42 Hugo Erfurth (German, 1874–1948). In the late 20th century, Erfurth's superb portraiture has been overshadowed by that of his countryman, August Sander. This is unfortunate, as Erfurth's work ranks among the finest of the century. Erfurth never entirely abandoned the soft-focus Pictorialist ethos, and never fully embraced the crisp tenets of Modernism. His portraits, often within landscapes, have a haunting and melancholy air. Here the ample floral adornment speaks of an equivalent womanhood. *See also 44.* Courtesy Museum Folkwang, Essen, Germany.
43 August Sander (German, 1876–1964). This portrait was made in the context of Sander's ambitious project to document German society, *Man in the Twentieth Century*, in which photographs of all social types would be included. Sander wanted his subjects shown 'in an environment corresponding to their own individuality'. By posing the two girls together, Sander tells us something of rural social mores *and* individual personality; the identical roses on the dresses speak of social expectations, the hand-held sprig of personal whim. Courtesy August Sander Archive, Sinzig, Germany.
44 Hugo Erfurth (German, 1874–1948). *See also 42.* Courtesy Agfa Foto Historama, and Museum Ludwig, Cologne.
45 Julia Margaret Cameron (British, 1815–1879). Cameron began her photographic career at the relatively late age of forty-eight, but she took to the medium with an astonishing facility, crafting an expressive style which is now seen to have anticipated the Pictorialist movement. Cameron staged elaborate tableaux, on literary, religious and mythological themes. In stagings featuring women, flowers – which she loved – played an indispensable role as symbols of spirituality, inner beauty, purity and love. Mrs Duckworth was the photographer's niece and the mother of Virginia Wolfe and Vanessa Bell. Courtesy © 1990 The Art Institute of Chicago, All rights reserved.
46 Thérèse Le Prat (French, 1895–1966). Le Prat was married to a well-known specialist of Khmer art. In 1937 she travelled to Indochina with her sister-in-law, the French photographer Denise Colomb, visiting Angkor, where this photograph was taken. Notable here is the striking relationship between the shapes of head and flower and the extraordinary delicacy with which the flower is handled. Courtesy Collection The Author, New York.
47 Cecil Beaton (British, 1904–1980). Courtesy The J. Paul Getty Museum, Malibu, California.
48 Michael Spano (American, b. 1949). In Spano's enigmatic portrait, the calla lily seems to be a part of the body rather than a separate object of adornment; its curves mirror those of the chin and its shadow; its texture is

one with the skin. Could it be another sense organ, like the eye, ear or nose, but attuned to messages from a fifth dimension? Courtesy Laurence Miller Gallery, New York.

49 Raymond Voinquel (French, b. 1912). Voinquel's lush blooms personify the actress Foun Sen, then at the peak of her career. Along with the traditional associations of beauty, love and perfection, the rose also speaks of secrecy and mystery – vestiges of its meaning in the Middle Ages before it was appropriated by the Church as an emblem of Mary's purity, glory and sorrow. Courtesy Kate Heller Gallery, London.

50 Robert Mapplethorpe (American, 1946–1989). Mapplethorpe died tragically of AIDS at the peak of his career, leaving a legacy of floral photographs (along with portraits and nudes) which compares favourably with the finest work of any period. Acutely sensitive to nuances of form and texture, and with the eye for detail which characterizes all great photographers, he produced floral studies that are elegant, stylized and overtly sexual. In this self-portrait of sorts, Mapplethorpe equates his own condition with that of the orchid – fragile, rare, exotic and solitary – and very much alone in the public eye. *See also 60, 127, 134, 175, 179.* Courtesy © The Estate of Robert Mapplethorpe, New York.

51 André Kertész (Hungarian, naturalized American, 1894–1985). Kertész gives us a 'portrait' of Piet Mondrian without the artist's physical presence: 'He simplified, simplified, simplified. The studio with its symmetry dictated the composition. He had a vase with a flower, but the flower was artificial. It was coloured by him with the right colour to match the studio.' It is the flower itself which animates the picture and personifies Mondrian's spirit. *See also 128.* Courtesy © Estate of André Kertész, New York, 1990.

52 Helen Levitt (American, b. 1918). Levitt has always had a particular empathy for city children. Here her young subject confronts the camera with a fierce possessiveness; the photographer, acutely sensitive to fortuitous relationships, captures the striking correspondence between the child's hand and the lily, thus reminding the viewer of the child's own delicacy and vulnerability. Courtesy Laurence Miller Gallery, New York.

53 Louis Faurer (American, b. 1916). Although Faurer earned his living as a fashion photographer, it was the street life of New York City that held him in thrall. 'My eyes search for people who are grateful for life,' he explained in 1979, 'whose enduring spirit is bathed by such piercing white light as to provide their present and future with hope.' Flowers contribute to several of Faurer's images. There is a certain poignancy to their presence in a Faurer scheme; unlike the grand, confident displays prepared by florists, these bouquets are pieced together from a few sprigs, bought by people with scant resources but for whom the flower is nevertheless a vital necessity, a beacon of hope. *See also 166.* Courtesy © Louis Faurer, New York.

54 Eikoh Hosoe (Japanese, b. 1933). *Barakei*, or *Ordeal by Roses*, was first published in 1963, a collaboration between the photographer Hosoe and the writer Yukio Mishima. The rose, first among the flowers which features in many of the images, is no passive symbol of beauty and purity, but a talisman, a weapon, and an ally not incapable of treachery; Mishima had even suggested *The Punishment of a Rose* as a possible title. Courtesy National Gallery of Canada, Ottawa.

55 Jean Dieuzaide (French, b. 1921). Artists enter the spirit of portraiture with an advantage over the ordinary subject: they can have an intuitive grasp of the photographer's intentions and can often visualize the finished result. Sometimes the artist will have his own agenda, and a weak photographer will have his image commandeered.

On other occasions the two will conspire to fabricate the portrait. Here, Dieuzaide works together with Salvador Dali, high priest of Surrealism, to transform Dali into a monster emerging from the deep, a monster with the most unlikely horns. Courtesy © Jean Dieuzaide, Toulouse, France.

56 Dennis Hopper (American, b. 1936). By contrast with Dieuzaide's portrait of Dali and Hosoe's portrayal of Mishima, both of which were staged, Hopper's image of Pop artist Andy Warhol, snapped during a restaurant meal in New York, is more of a diaristic notation. The flower was simply *there*, a given, but the two have made much of it, with Warhol leaning into the flower to split the image or stress symmetries, and Hopper cleverly framing the picture in such a way that the flower functions as the artist's eyebrows. A striking feature of the image is the contrast between the open flower and Warhol's closed demeanour. Courtesy © Dennis Hopper, Santa Monica, California.

57 Arnold Newman (American, b. 1918). Arnold Newman was given the task of making a portrait of an artist known for his *own* brilliant photography which deals obsessively with notions of self. Flowers play a significant role in Lucas Samaras's oeuvre, and Newman has ingeniously introduced the theme by placing Samaras behind his own semi-transparent floral shirt and lining up the centre of one flower with the artist's eye, thus signifying a visionary artist. Courtesy © Arnold Newman, New York.

58 Imogen Cunningham (American, 1883–1976). Of all Cunningham's flower studies, which date from the mid-1920s to the mid-1930s, this angular graphic design, almost devoid of half-tones, is perhaps closest in spirit to the machine aesthetic which fascinated so many forward-thinking photographers in Europe and America between the wars.

Cunningham was well informed about this aesthetic at home and abroad, and was familiar with the work of Blossfeldt and Renger-Patzsch from the periodical *Das Deutsche Lichtbild* and from their books. *See also 77, 174.* Courtesy The Imogen Cunningham Trust, Berkeley, California.

59 Yasuhiro Ishimoto (Japanese, b. 1921). Ishimoto's extensive flower images of a host of familiar and exotic varieties were published in 1989 in *Hana* (Flower) (Chronicle Books, San Francisco). Ishimoto owes a debt to Cunningham's sharp focus, tight cropping and almost microscopic clarity, but he is, generally speaking, less interested in design. This image is one of a series on the southern magnolia, which depicts the flower both in detail and in its entirety. *See also 62.* Courtesy © Yasuhiro Ishimoto, Tokyo.

60 Robert Mapplethorpe (American, 1946–1989). Mapplethorpe worked extensively with flowers. Unlike Cunningham, however, he had little or no interest in the flower in nature; his interest was unabashedly decorative, formal, and metaphorical – there is clearly a connection between his flowers and the strong human bodies he so sensuously renders. *See also 50, 127, 134, 175, 179.* Courtesy © The Estate of Robert Mapplethorpe, New York.

61 John Atchley (American, dates unknown). With its soft gradations of greys, this image might easily be confused with a pencil drawing. Atchley has given us much more than a close look at the interior of a flower; somehow the forms he has unveiled evoke human shapes, or perhaps a passage through some mysterious cave, promising some revelation at its centre. Courtesy © John Atchley; Polaroid Collection, Cambridge, Massachusetts.

62 Yasuhiro Ishimoto (Japanese, b. 1921). *See also 59.* Courtesy © Yasuhiro Ishimoto, Tokyo.

63 Denis Brihat (French, b. 1928). For more than thirty

years Brihat has devoted himself to the study of nature, which he believes is in some way a 'civilization parallel to our own'. The black tulip was the subject of a 3-year study, stopped only when the bulbs stopped growing. Where Atchley (61) has played on the grey scale, Brihat gives us an almost calligraphic image of rich blacks, a quality enhanced by unique *re*developmental procedures that he has worked out in the darkroom. *See also 161.* Courtesy © Denis Brihat, Bonnieux, France.

64 Konrad Cramer (German, naturalized American, 1888–1963). Cramer took up residence in the United States as a young man. He was a painter, deeply influenced by the avant-garde group known later as Blaue Reiter. He brought his love of abstraction to photography, arguing that 'photography is not only a "making of pictures" but a training in deeper and wider seeing, which gives to its practitioners a greater happiness and fuller enjoyment of life as their eyes are opened to new horizons' (Heather Alberts, *Image* 29 (1): 3–4). A rose allowed for this 'thinking and feeling in form and rhythm'. Courtesy Collection Leonard and Marjorie Vernon, Los Angeles.

65 Jerry Uelsmann (American, b. 1934). Uelsmann is best known for his haunting composite imagery with its Symbolist concerns. But many photographs, he explains, 'seem complete when I click the shutter'. Such is the image shown here, taken the day after an unexpected hard freeze in northern Florida. 'Above all else', he has noted, 'the camera is a license to explore . . . The mere possession of a camera tends to heighten our perceptual awareness.' *See also 155.*

66 Scowen & Co. (Ceylon, active 1870s to 1890s). The firm maintained high standards, technically and pictorially. The work of Charles T. Scowen, the founder, must have been very accomplished before he arrived in Ceylon in the early 1870s, notes John Falconer in an essay on 19th-century photography in the colony (*The Photographic Collector* 2 [Summer, 1981]: 39), 'for the quality of his work demonstrates considerable skill: the beautifully lit and simply composed studies of racial types, and the fine landscapes and plant studies at Peradeniya [the botanical garden] argue a longer familiarity with the medium.' Courtesy Collection William L. Schaeffer, Chester, Connecticut. *See also 18, 19, 69.*

67 Cay Lang (American, b. 1948). Since the early 1980s Lang has worked with the subject of the dead and dying flower, which she sees as a metaphor for the human condition. She writes: 'When they are young all tulips look essentially the same, but as they grow older, they begin to develop individual personalities. Their range of response extends from immediately dropping over and acquiescing, to actively resisting by pushing outward, to wrapping their petals around each other in what appears to be an embrace . . . Flowers seem particularly sensitive to each other's presence, and appear to create a community when cut and placed in a bowl. They seem to be drawn to some flowers and repelled by others, and will rearrange themselves according to these affinities and resistances.' When certain *individual* flowers stand out for their force of 'personality', they become, as with *Ophelia*, candidates for portraiture. Courtesy © Cay Lang, San Francisco, California.

68 Chris Enos (American, b. 1944). Like Lang, Enos is drawn to the subject of the dying flower, but she takes a very different approach; it is not 'personality' which intrigues her but the revelations of form, colour and texture as the life force ebbs. For her studies Enos used the 20 × 24" Polaroid camera, with its superb clarity of detail. She reveals a turbulent aspect of nature which has no precedence in art. *See also 181.* Courtesy © Chris Enos, Boston, Massachusetts.

69 Scowen & Co. (Ceylon, active 1870s to 1890s). *See*

also *18, 19, 66*. Courtesy Collection Olivia and John Parker, Manchester, Massachusetts.

70 Emmanuel Sougez (French, 1889–1972). *See also 75*. Courtesy © 1990 The Art Institute of Chicago, Julien Levy Collection, Gift of Jean Levy and the Estate of Julien Levy.

71 Alma Lavenson (American, 1897–1989). There is a breathtaking monumentality to this chrysanthemum which may remind the viewer of O'Keeffe's painted imagery. What is unique to the photograph, however, is a sense of nature's awesome power, the magnitude of the struggle for life in what we usually think of as a rather demure flower. Like her friend Imogen Cunningham, Lavenson was a member of the West Coast's Modernist group known as *F64*, which championed a vigorous, purist approach, a search, in Weston's words, for 'the quintessence revealed direct'. Lavenson is not content with surface appearances, but closes in on the essential structure, much as she did with her primary subject – architecture. Courtesy Collection Susan Ehrens, Berkeley, © Alma Lavenson Associates.

72 Charles Sheeler (American, 1883–1965). Sheeler's perfectionism, unfailing sense of composition, and erudition in matters of art history combine in his exceptional flower photographs. Whereas his *Zinnia and Nasturtium Leaves* (124) played on the notion of the Dutch flower piece, this image is indebted to the Japanese print; Sheeler was deeply impressed with the quality of flatness and the aura of serenity characteristic of the Utamoro prints and Japanese folding screen he kept in this studio. Courtesy Amon Carter Museum, Fort Worth, Texas. *See also 124*.

73 Edwin Hale Lincoln (American, 1848–1938). Lincoln published his magnificent oeuvre, *Wildflowers of New England*, in parts, between 1910 and 1914. These images, printed masterfully in platinum, show the flowers whole and in their natural surroundings, although for the sake of control over the lighting he would often transport plants to his studio. He refused to disclose the source of his plants for fear that flower lovers would 'tear my friends up by the roots'. Today, Lincoln's work languishes in libraries, but it deserves a better fate. Courtesy The New York Public Library.

74 Edward Steichen (American, 1879–1973), Steichen's *Lotus, Mount Kisco* was made in 1915, the year following his return to the United States from France, where, since 1910, he had involved himself in the study of genetics and experimentation with hybridization at his Voulangis gardens. Mount Kisco was the home of Mrs Eugene Meyer, a collector of avant-garde art and a supporter of forward looking photography – it was she who had commissioned Sheeler to make an extensive study of her estate. In this image, Steichen has wisely suppressed the natural inclination to fill the frame with the flower, realizing that its richness needed a foil, which he provides with foliage. *See also 11, 14, 15, 100–103; p. 19*. Courtesy National Gallery of Canada, Ottawa.

75 Emmanuel Sougez (French, 1889–1972). While Steichen's lotus is provided with a natural foil, Sougez's rose is offset with a man-made object, a plate perhaps. Sougez seems to have been searching for some human connection, something beyond the realism championed by Renger-Patzsch and others. His images often include some evidence that the cut flower is a human artefact as much as a natural object. *See also 70*. Courtesy Gilman Paper Company Collection, New York.

76 E. F. Kitchen (American, b. 1951). Kitchen is a well-established commercial photographer for whom the flower functions both as a prop for portraiture and as a subject in its own right. She has printed a number of her flower images in platinum in order fully to exploit the grey scale; in this, and in showing the flower whole, she is following in the footsteps of Lincoln. Her interest, however,

is aesthetic. Courtesy © E. F. Kitchen, Venice, California.

77 Imogen Cunningham (American, 1883–1976). Cunningham's magnolia is one of the best known of 20th-century flower photographs. It is seen lucidly, in the best *F64* tradition, entirely filling the frame. Its blend of crisp representation and soft abstraction is such that the flower would be almost unidentifiable were it not for the central structure of pistil and stamens (what the photographer called in a further close-up, *Tower of Jewels*). This dynamic tension gives the image its lasting attraction. *Formen einer Blume*, as it was originally called, was one of the 10 images chosen by Weston for inclusion in the seminal German exhibition *Film und Foto*. With some irritation Cunningham later complained: 'Some people think I never did another flower.' *See also 58, 174*. Courtesy © The Imogen Cunningham Trust, Berkeley, California.

78 Alinari Studio (Italian; **Giuseppe Alinari**, 1836–1890; **Leopoldo Alinari**, 1832–1865; **Romualdo Alinari**, 1830–1891). It is hard to believe that this image was made in the 1870s; one might well assume it to be a close cousin to a Sougez or a Cunningham. Nothing is known of the specific intentions of the photographer in this instance, other than that the firm of Alinari was a commercial concern with a wide variety of subjects available in various sizes and formats. Most likely the intention was didactic, since the photograph shows the morning glory in various states of bloom and from various perspectives. *See also 121*. Courtesy Collection William L. Schaeffer, Chester, Connecticut.

79 Anonymous photographer (active early 1900s). The flower girl is a popular motif in 19th-century art and literature, usually standing for unsullied innocence. In a story told by the popular writer Alphonse Karr, for instance, a flower girl, weary of being chased by men, 'who clasp me by the waist and call me Flora's priestess', resolves to flee from mankind and revert to her original condition, 'that of a simple flower'. But the buxom young woman shown here is a bird of another feather, promising sensual delights of a fairly specific nature. For a gentleman fluent in the language of flowers, however, the message holds a contradictory meaning: an inverted flower stands for denial! Courtesy © Uwe Scheid Collection, Uberherrn/Saar, Germany.

80 Anonymous photographer (active 1920s). Throughout the 19th and 20th centuries, it is women who have customarily been depicted as flowers (and, conversely, flowers have been personified as women). Flowers are vulnerable and fragile creatures and their beauty is short-lived. As these qualities corresponded to conventional perceptions of women, flowers were readily adopted as symbols. The language of flowers evolved and refined these symbols to a near ludicrous degree. It was also 'understood' that women were naturally more sensitive (and more susceptible) to their charms. Courtesy © Uwe Scheid Collection, Uberherrn/Saar, Germany.

81 Wilhelm von Gloeden (German, 1856–1931). Like many other poets and painters of his generation, Baron von Gloeden imagined a romantic past free from the horrors of the industrial age, a time of endless philosophical speculation and Platonic love, sweet music and flowers, not to mention beautiful young boys; but from another perspective, the theatre of the antique was a necessary cloak for his homoerotic desires. Private collection, New York.

82 Charles Adrien (French, ?–1930). Courtesy Société Française de Photographie, Paris.

83 Henri Bergon (French, 1863–1912). Perhaps the charm of this picture derives from its uncertain intentions, as if the photographer could not quite decide on its true subject – the still life or the nude: in this regard, it is poles apart from Adrien's confident study. It is also far more blatant in its erotic thrust, with the photographer

revealing more of his lascivious intent than he might have cared to realize. Courtesy Société Française de Photographie, Paris.

84–86 Anonymous photographer (French, active early 1900s). The picture postcard emerged in Europe in 1869 and went on to enjoy an immense popularity which has never abated. Flowers were ubiquitous, standing in for the real thing at an infinitesimal fraction of the price. Series of images like this one were popular as the cards could be sent individually over a period of time. Courtesy Collection The Author, New York.

87 E. J. Bellocq (American, 1873–1949). In the 1910s Bellocq, a commercial photographer working in New Orleans, undertook a series of portraits of the women of a Storyville brothel. His intentions are not known. It is possible that he had some kind of commercial exploitation in mind, perhaps a reference book for the brothel's clientele, but equally possible that he was driven by some private impulse. However, there is nothing prurient in his approach, the pictures are compassionate and in good taste. In this particular portrait the roses function, in a literary sense, as both analogy and metaphor: the subject's mature beauty is like a rose; and the rose stands for passionate love.

The silver print on printing-out paper was made by Lee Friedlander from Bellocq's original plate. Courtesy Minneapolis Institute of Arts, Minnesota; © Lee Friedlander, New York.

88 Sally Mann (American, b. 1951). Mann's fluid study of a child's legs adorned with gooseneck loosestrife makes no reference to time or place: it might have as easily been envisioned by F. Holland Day a hundred years earlier. But Mann does not propose a fabulous antiquity, simply the joy of the human body in the here-and-now. Courtesy Sally Mann, Lexington, Virginia.

89 Frederick Holland Day (American, 1864–1933). Courtesy The Royal Photographic Society, Bath.

90 František Drtikol (Czech, 1883–1961). Drtikol's nude makes for an illuminating comparison with Bellocq's; both employ a lush grouping of roses to signify desire. But whereas an artless simplicity and directness are the key to Bellocq's force, pictorial and symbolic sophistication define the Drtikol. Note, for example, how the body and floral arrangement echo each other, as do breast and petal. Bellocq's women are earthy, sensual creatures promising physical pleasure; Drtikol's nudes are the archetypes of dreams. Courtesy National Gallery of Canada. Gift of International Museum of Photography at George Eastman House, Rochester, New York.

91 Bert Stern (American, b. 1929). Bert Stern's unabashed depiction of the actress leaves no doubt in our minds as to what the rose signifies for her. In *The Last Sitting* (1982), Stern observed, 'Marilyn Monroe is the first American goddess – our goddess of love. We created her just as much as she created herself. She arose in response to our sexual yearning and our spiritual awakening. She is gone but she is everywhere . . . Through the magic of photography the light from Marilyn Monroe is still reaching us.' Courtesy © Bert Stern, New York.

92 Wendell MacRae (American, 1896–1980). For Outerbridge, Day and Lynes, the flower is an agent inducing bliss or lassitude. By contrast, MacRae's flowers, borne on the arms of a female Mercury, signify an active, energizing force. Before MacRae took up photography in the 1930s he had worked as a film editor, and before that as a film researcher; possibly the sense of movement he so effectively conveys derives from this cinematic sensibility. Courtesy Witkin Gallery, New York.

93, 95 Paul Outerbridge (American, 1896–1958). Outerbridge had an enduring interest in flowers. He enjoyed the challenge of the still life , and his nudes were often embellished by real or artificial flowers, or shown against backdrops of floral wallpapers and fabrics. But as unconventional as his flowers are in *pictorial* terms, symbolically they follow mainstream convention, as emblems of femininity, beauty, perfection, and so on.

In fairness to the photographer, it should be noted that the first of these pictures was originally a Carbro-colour image made from a glass plate; however, this was not available for reproduction, and it must be admitted that a certain expressive aspect is missing. Outerbridge considered the Carbro process the finest means available of producing work in colour. *See also 130.* Courtesy Graham Howe, Curatorial Assistance, Pasadena, California.

94 George Platt Lynes (American, 1907–1955). Today, Lynes is much admired for his Surrealist-inspired portraiture and homoerotic nudes. Whereas many of his colleagues seemed to have adopted Surrealism superficially as a style, he seems to have grasped its essence more profoundly. Between 1936 and 1940 Lynes undertook an extensive series on the theme of the Greek myth, from which *Narcissus* is drawn. Courtesy Ehlers Caudill Gallery, Chicago.

96–98 Elisabeth Sunday (American, b. 1958). Desire of a kind other than the erotic is characteristic of Sunday's figure and flower diptychs and triptychs. These images stem from dreams: her discovery of a painting by her grandfather of the Mengbetu people, with their elongated heads, seems to have triggered lucid dreams in which vegetal forms evolved before her eyes, and elongated human figures materialized, thinning upwards into clouds and raining down upon the earth. Moved by these vivid images, Sunday determined to register them photographically, finding in a distorting mirror an effective means of representing this upward/downward cycle – *ergo* man's interdependence with the vegetal world. In using distortion she risked transformations which would appear silly or grotesque, but to her credit the technique is used with sensitivity and taste. Courtesy ©️ Elisabeth Sunday, San Francisco.

99 Anonymous photographer. Nothing much of the original surface of the photograph shows through in this charming picture. That the face survives is notable: the painter seems to have realized when the expressive potential of the brush must yield to the descriptive powers of the lens. Courtesy Gordon L. Bennett Collection, Kentfield, California.

100–103 Edward Steichen (American, 1879–1973). We think of Steichen's floral imagery, colour or black-and-white, in terms of a rather straightforward approach, and so his experimental work may come somewhat as a surprise. But Steichen had always experimented with printing techniques; in his early days as a Pictorialist he had worked primarily with platinum and gum-bichromate processes, often masterfully combining the two. Later he employed cyanotype, Autochrome, and various colour processes such as the dye imbibition method shown here. *See also 11, 14, 15, 74; p. 19.*

104 Marvin Gasoi (Canadian, b. 1949). Courtesy ©️ Marvin Gasoi; Art 45, Montreal.

105 Keiichi Tahara (Japanese, b. 1951). There are as many ways of cultivating photographic hybrids as there are inventive photographers. Keiichi Tahara has developed a unique method (the secret of which he guards), which produces a dazzling decorative effect as a ground for his floral subjects. Tahara has long been fascinated by transparency, mounting his images on large sheets of glass or clear plastic. Undoubtedly his dramatic colour effects are a consequence of his early experience as a lighting designer. Courtesy ©️ Keiichi Tahara, Paris.

106 Lucas Samaras (Greek, naturalized American, 1936). Lucas Samaras's elasticized flower arrangement is a one-of-a-kind assemblage of Polaroid imagery. Each of his *Panoramas*, of which this is an example, was composed of a number of single images of the same subject matter, cut into strips and reassembled. The effect was twofold: to lend a certain monumentality and unfamiliarity to ordinary objects (but not beyond the point of recognizability); and to conflate several disparate moments in time, thus confounding our notion of the very 'instant' which Polaroid purported to capture.

Floral elements had figured in Samaras's earlier works as well. In a series called *Photo-Transformations* of a decade earlier, for example, he had portrayed himself in his kitchen being attacked and devoured by a renegade bouquet. In other images, floral schemes of a Byzantine brilliance illuminate what curator Peter Weiermair has called his 'soliloquies'. Thus Arnold Newman's floral portrayal of the artist is a fitting one (57). Courtesy ©️ Lucas Samaras; Pace/MacGill Gallery, New York.

107 Starn twins (Doug and Mike Starn, American, b. 1961). A certain iconoclasm marks the composite approach of the Starn twins. In very recent years they have ruffled a few feathers in the world of art photography by scratching, tearing, staining, taping and otherwise assaulting their materials. In the art world, however, they have been heralded as new romantics and visionaries, 'reinvesting the photograph with the qualities of personal touch, (apparent) historical pedigree and private expressivity,' as one critic wrote. In true 'deconstructionist' spirit, their frankly nostalgic subject matter, rife with historical allusion, is never allowed to break free of its means of representation. Courtesy ©️ Starn twins; Stux Gallery, New York.

108 Stefan De Jaeger (Belgian, b. 1957). The 'instant' nature of Polaroid materials allowed De Jaeger to build up his picture as a painter would, making aesthetic decisions at each of the 26 stages. The method gave him great flexibility, allowing him to choose a novel point at various distances from the subject each time he made an exposure. Like others who invented composite techniques, De Jaeger sought to break from the conventional frame; the two images on the sides are a reminder of the open-endedness of the technique.

The 'Sam' acknowledged here is the late Sam Wagstaff, a distinguished curator and collector who organized an exhibition of flower photography, which included De Jaeger's composite image, at the Detroit Institute of Arts in 1985. Courtesy ©️ Stefan De Jaeger, Brussels.

109 David Lebe (American, b. 1948). David Lebe began his light drawings in 1976, thinking them a natural means of photography, and in no way 'unique or experimental'. Lebe uses ambient light to record a basic arrangement of objects, then intervenes with a penlight, over exposures ranging from one minute to one hour, to trace the contours of the actual objects, or, as in this image, to freely express his imagination. The prints are later hand-coloured. Thus the works are a synthesis of drawing, photography and painting. 'He has invented systems that enable him to create images on his own terms, freed from photography's realistic mandate,' notes critic Thomas Gartside (*Arts Magazine*, October, 1985), who also underlines the connection between Lebe's work and the photogram technique of Moholy-Nagy: 'In both bodies of work the artist is performing with light to express his fantasy.' Courtesy ©️ David Lebe, Philadelphia.

110 Pierre Boogaerts (Canadian and Belgian, b. 1946). Courtesy ©️ Pierre Boogaerts, Montreal.

111 Rick Hock (American, b. 1947). Hock's training as a printmaker is evident in his *Codex* series. Each *Codex* is 'a visual text, not only to be seen, but also read; to me they are pages for an encyclopaedic book of images that is ever evolving'. Hock's found images are copied on 35mm slides, then printed, and then, through a Polaroid process, transferred to paper, one image at a time, on to a grid of either 28 or 36 related images. For Hock, meaning is open-ended, and he encourages personal interpretation. Courtesy Hallmark Photographic Collection, Hallmark Cards, Inc, Kansas City, Missouri. ©️ Rick Hock, Rochester, New York.

112 Gordon L. Bennett (American, b. 1933). Bennett has long been a collector of photographs, but he has also produced a number of collages in which a floral theme predominates. For *Return* he addresses the theme of time: a 20th-century postcard connects with an 18th-century engraving, and the living flower with the fossil remains. The idea of boundaries, and breaking them, is also addressed in the connection between the print and the card, and in the way the card breaks out of its mount. Courtesy ©️ Gordon L. Bennett, Kentfield, California.

113 Olivia Parker (American, b. 1941). *See also 143.* Courtesy ©️ Olivia Parker, Manchester, Massachusetts.

114 Francis J. Bruguière (American, 1879–1945). Like so many other photographers of his time, Bruguière started as a Pictorialist, but after 1913 shifted to 'straight' photography and then into the mode of experimental abstraction for which he is celebrated today – multiple exposures and light patterns of a purely abstract nature made by arranging and lighting cut paper. This multiple exposure of a lily tries to arrive at the essence of the flower through a Cubist multiplicity of simultaneous visions. This print was made by James Enyeart from the photographer's original negative. Courtesy International Museum of Photography at George Eastman House, Rochester, New York.

115 Suzanne Opton (American, b. 1945). Like Bruguière (114), Opton is determined to get beyond conventional approaches to the still life, and the tyranny of surface appearance. In a conventional studio portrayal the gladioli would have been placed in front of a neutral, featureless backdrop. What Opton has done, in effect, is to cut up this backdrop and insert it at will behind individual blossoms, so that the single image contains, as it were, a number of individual still-lifes. Courtesy ©️ Suzanne Opton, New York.

116 Baron Adolf de Meyer (French, 1868–1946). This photogram follows in the tradition of Schad, Moholy-Nagy and Man Ray, who were employing the technique in the early 1920s. It appears to be made from a negative image of a three-dimensional object, or possibly in combination with one. In any event, it points to a Modernist side of Meyer's work that has gone unnoticed. *See also 122, 123.* Courtesy The Addison Gallery of American Art, Phillips Academy, Andover, Massachusetts.

117 Man Ray (American, 1890–1976). Rayographs were produced with various techniques. Sometimes Man Ray would immerse the objects in the developer while the exposure was taking place. Also, the light source might be held steady or it might be moved, creating a rich penumbra. Man Ray did not actually invent the technique: Talbot's photogenic drawing and Bayard's direct-positive method were true photograms. Moreover, Christian Schad and László Moholy-Nagy had developed the idea more or less contemporaneously with Man Ray. But for the artists of the 1920s, the technique was a true invention in the sense of its expressivity. *See also 173.* Courtesy The Museum of Modern Art, New York. Gift of James Thrall Soby.

118 Walter Peterhans (German, naturalized American, 1897–1960). As head of the photography programme at the Bauhaus in Dessau, a programme which he himself established, Peterhans was one of the prime exponents of 'the New Objectivity'. He was preparing his students for careers in commerce and advertising, and his own image sets a high standard for studies of texture and contrast. Colour may also have been a point of the exercise: Peterhans was probably demonstrating how different colours translated into black and white. Exercise aside, one cannot deny that there is a lyric poetry to the image. It stands as a paradigm of Bauhaus principle, which was to marry artistic expression, scientific knowledge and solid craftsmanship to 20th-century techniques of mass production. The image is one of ten from a portfolio. Courtesy San Francisco Museum of Modern Art, Mrs Ferdinand C. Smith Fund Purchase.

119 Martin Gerlach (Austrian, dates unknown). In the late 19th century the plant reigned supreme as a source of ornament and design. Gerlach's decorative alphabet was intended as a source, but most designers preferred the stylized, geometric patterns available in such books as Eugène Grasset's *La Plante et ses applications ornementales* (1896). Gerlach's arrangements appear informal but were in fact painstakingly contrived.

Collotype, Gerlach's process, is a bichromate process for obtaining high-quality ink reproduction of photographic images, almost indistinguishable from actual photographs. Courtesy The Museum of Modern Art, New York.

120 Heinrich Kühn (Austrian, 1866–1944). A certain spareness, or what Beaumont Newhall has called 'posterlike composition', characterizes Kühn's exceptional still-lifes, hinting at the coming modernity.

Kühn was one of Europe's foremost Pictorialists, and a master of the difficult gum bichromate method which was much admired for its impressionistic effect. A December 1906 issue of *Camerawork* reported, 'His pictures clearly show the result of his special methods. The proportion of the light and colour-values is frequently so truly reproduced that we feel the sensation of colour . . .' Courtesy © Uwe Scheid Collection, Überherrn/Saar, Germany. *See also 16.*

121 Alinari Studio (Italian; **Giuseppe**, 1836–1890; **Leopoldo**, 1832–1865; **Romualdo**, 1830–1891). *See also 78.* Courtesy William L. Schaeffer, Chester, Connecticut.

122 Baron Adolf de Meyer (French, 1868–1946). De Meyer professed to be merely a hobbiest when it came to photography, but in fact he took his work very seriously indeed, joining the influential Linked Ring in London and exhibiting in their salon in 1898 and later, in 1907 and 1912, at Stieglitz's 291 in New York. In a letter to Stieglitz he specifically requested that his works be shown as a body and not mixed in with those of Steichen, White and Kasebier. *See also 116, 123.* Courtesy Staley Wise Gallery, New York.

123 Baron Adolf de Meyer (French, 1868–1946) *See also 116, 122.* Photogravure from *Camera Work*, No. 24, October 1908. Courtesy Minneapolis Institute of Arts, Minnesota.

124 Charles Sheeler (American, 1883–1965). This study might be seen as a modern, minimal equivalent of the 17th-century Dutch flower piece. It has something too of the contemporary fixation with the insistent new technologies that were radically transforming life – the zinnia stands unnaturally upright, like a radio beacon.

(There is some dispute over the date of this picture. Traditionally it has been dated 1915, but Theodore Stebbins and Norman Keyes, Jr., authors of *Charles Sheeler: The Photographs* (New York Graphic Society, 1987), feel that a 1916–17 date better corresponds to the photographer's 'rich period of discovery and growth'). *See also 72.* Courtesy Worcester Art Museum, Worcester, Massachusetts.

125 Jan Groover (American, b. 1943). Courtesy Robert Miller Gallery, New York; © Jan Groover, New York.

126 Marta Hoepffner (German, b. 1912). Hoepffner was one of the avant-garde photographers who emerged in Germany in the 1930s. She is best known today for her photograms produced as homage to the work of Manuel de Falla and Wassily Kandinsky. In her early years she had studied with the painter Willi Baumeister, from whom she learned the language of abstraction. Courtesy Jane Corkin Gallery, Toronto.

127 Robert Mapplethorpe (American, 1946–1989). These active, indeed aggressive, flowers which protrude ominously from their container have an animal vitality wholly unlike their docile cousins in the conventional still-life; their sideways thrust is balanced by the dramatic upward sweep of the surface on which the bowl rests. As Alan Hollinghurst has observed, 'Like Edward Weston's polished peppers, Mapplethorpe's flowers are subjected to a scrutiny which discovers their tense sensuality. Their staring eyes, their extended fingers, their drooping or thrusting penile leaves complement the concentrated postures of Mapplethorpe's men' (*Robert Mapplethorpe, 1970–1983*, London, 1983, p. 17). *See also 50, 60, 134, 175, 179.* Courtesy © The Estate of Robert Mapplethorpe, New York.

128 André Kertész (Hungarian, naturalized American, 1894–1985). Although Kertész most often made straightforward use of the medium, with the camera and in the darkroom, he was drawn to the theme of distortion, as we see subtly engineered here, or wildly so in his extensive series on the nude. This interest seems to have dated from an early 'naturally' distorted image from 1917, *Underwater Swimmer*. As critic Hilton Cramer remarked in his introductory essay to *Distortions* (New York, 1976), 'Kertész's images, though often close to the frontiers of abstraction, always remain securely enclosed in an observable universe.' *See also 51.* Courtesy Estate of André Kertész, New York, © 1990.

129 Gérald Ducimetière (French, dates unknown). In this homage to Frank Lloyd Wright, Ducimetière finds an extraordinary correspondence between the form of the calla lily and the spiral architecture of the Guggenheim Museum. By working on the dark side of the gallery, he brings out this flower-like aspect of the Museum's interior structure. As for the lilies, they have been most ingeniously lit. Courtesy Collection The Author, New York.

130 Paul Outerbridge (American, 1896–1958). For the most part, Outerbridge's flowers were arrangements in vases. He had no interest in an out-of-doors naturalism, nor in the kind of reductivist abstractions characteristic of Cunningham. (There is one exception to this, an extreme close-up of a calla lily titled *Abstraction*, 1924). He took extraordinary pains to refine his compositions. *See also 93, 94.* Courtesy Marjorie and Leonard Vernon Collection, Los Angeles. Permission of G. Ray Hawkins Gallery, Los Angeles.

131 Rosalind Maingot (British, dates unknown). The flower piece photographed by Rosalind Maingot at mid-20th century would have been favourably reviewed by a European critic of the 18th or 19th centuries. Although the composition has been carefully arranged, it convinces us of its informality, and there is the required fallen blossom representing the inevitability of death and decay in traditional *vanitas* symbolism – that is, the transience of our own lives. Courtesy The Royal Photographic Society, Bath.

132 Don Worth (American, b. 1924). Courtesy © Copyright 1985, Don Worth, Mill Valley California. Witkin Gallery, New York.

133 Sheila Metzner (American, b. 1939). Metzner finds the perfect foil for her frilly, ultra-feminine orchid in the stolid but handsome 'Mondrian' vase; it is almost as if a prima ballerina is lifted on the shoulders of her robust male partner. A languid sensuality pervades all

Metzner's flower pictures: 'stilled life', as poet Mark Strand described them in Metzner's book, *Objects of Desire*, New York, 1986. Courtesy © Sheila Metzner, New York.

134 Robert Mapplethorpe (American, 1946–1989). *See also 50, 60, 127, 175, 179.* Courtesy © The Estate of Robert Mapplethorpe, New York.

135 Steve Lovi (American, b. 1939). Lovi is a commercial photographer who has created an extensive series of floral greetings cards which tease the viewer with *illusions* (are the flowers real or printed?), and *allusions* (are we looking at painting, or watercolour?). Lovi was trained as a painter, and brings a superb sense of complementary colour to his work. Courtesy © Steve Lovi, London.

136 Morgan Whitney (American, 1869–1913). Music, Chinese carved stone and porcelain, automobiles, architecture and photography were some of the interests of Morgan Whitney, a member of a wealthy and prominent New Orleans family. Along with documentary imagery depicting architectural and rural subjects, Whitney tapped a more romantic vein with his still lifes, in which he combined his treasured Chinese objects with flowers which grew locally. Courtesy New Orleans Museum of Art: Gift of Mr and Mrs Morgan Whitney.

137 Hans Bellmer (German, 1902–1975). The female mannequin was a recurrent motif in the work of a number of Surrealist photographers, including Raoul Ubac, Umbo, Paul Outerbridge and Paul Citroen. Bellmer explored and developed the motif to the extent of making a life-size, articulated doll, which could assume a range of poses from the normal to the bizarre. Angst and eroticism pervade these works, and flowers play their role as emblems of erotic love. In this image, the neat arrangement suggests a wreath for a departed soul. Courtesy Leland Rice Collection, Berkeley, California.

138 Anonymous photographer. A Victorian domestic theatrical pageant seems to be the subject of this little tintype, In which a monstrous flower, quite crudely grafted on to its stem, is worshipped by a bevy of young women. Floral symbolism figured strongly in 19th-century popular and serious literature. Courtesy Palmquist Collection, Arcata, California.

139 Anonymous photographer. Screens similar to this still exist today at British seaside resorts. The tintype is an inexpensive but hardy little photograph which enjoyed wide popularity in the 19th century. Courtesy Palmquist Collection, Arcata, California.

140, 141 Joan Fontcuberta (Spanish, b. 1955). Courtesy Zabriskie Gallery, New York, © Joan Fontcuberta.

142 John Stezaker (British, b. 1949). A noted conceptual artist with a penchant for haunting hallucinatory visions, Stezaker has long been occupied with found photographic imagery and the technique of collage. Along with advertisements, movie stills, images from mothercare magazines and the like, postcards have presented a particularly rich vein. Combining babies and flowers, he conjures up a nightmarish realm of childhood terror and powerlessness. *See also p. 9.* Courtesy © John Stezaker; Salama-Caro Gallery, London.

143 Olivia Parker (American, b. 1941). Parker has always exhibited a deep, but qualified, respect for human culture. In *Stairway*, produced in the Polaroid 20 × 24″ studio in New York (photographers are invited to use the facilities, which they cannot own) she has fabricated an allegorical image which addresses this respect. For all of culture's uplifting force (represented most fundamentally by the stairway; enriched by the mathematical model, a Renaissance contrivance), it has also served to distance us from nature (signified by the flowers); only threads of this connection remain. The Adam and Eve figures (which appear, incidentally, in a number of Parker's works), are not meant to be understood in their literal sense as first human beings, but figuratively, as archetypes standing for every one of us. The stairway is a particularly hopeful metaphor, implying as it does movement in both directions. *See also 113*. Courtesy © Olivia Parker, Manchester, Massachusetts.

144 Gilbert & George (British; b. 1943, b. 1942). An astonishing number of artworks by Gilbert & George, the performance artists (or 'Living Sculptures', as they have described themselves), make use of floral tropes: *A Touch of Blossom*, 1971; *Gilbert & George in the Rhododendron Dell, Kew Gardens, London*, 1972; *Two Heads*, 1980 (in which two chrysanthemums personify the artists); *England*, 1980; *Bloom*, 1984, are only a few examples. Indeed, Gilbert & George seem intent on resuscitating the venerable 'language of flowers', with which the Victorians expressed ideas and emotions too dangerous to be put directly in words. In their updated prose they express a wide range of ideas and emotions: life and death, abundance, love, lust, narcissism, youth, beauty. In *Various Loves*, the calla lily, or arum, speaks of a promiscuous homosexuality. Courtesy Anthony d'Offay Gallery, London.

145 Georges Hugnet (French, 1906–1974). Hugnet's photocollage presents a disturbing image of sexual perversity. Mysterious rites of initiation take place within some sort of subterranean tunnel. The gigantic flower's tightly wrapped petals conceal the mystery within just as the hooded priests hide the true meaning of the rites from the *uninitiated*, i.e., the viewers. In this interpretation the flower reads as a grotesque emblem of a cult. Courtesy San Francisco Museum of Modern Art, Gift of Dr and Mrs Allan Roos.

146 Betty Hahn (American, b. 1940). Hahn employs camera vision as a point of departure; the photographic image is nothing more than a foundation for an expressive, gestural interpretation which utilizes a variety of traditional and non-traditional photographic processes – cyanotype, vandyke (like the cyanotype, but brown-toned), watercolour, chalk, pastels and, in what must be one of the most unusual marriages of materials, coloured thread stitched to gum bichromate prints (the knots of which represent flowers). In the image shown here Hahn uses watercolour effectively to convey – less literally and more evocatively – the essence of the iris's distinctive colouring. Courtesy © Betty Hahn, Albuquerque, New Mexico.

147 Barbara Crane (American, b. 1928). 'Enarc' is Crane spelled backwards, underlining Crane's intention, which is to address matters of perception rather than accept vision as an absolute or given. Crane's startling vision of the world is not born of manipulation of the image in a darkroom, but of standard photographic techniques applied in novel and ingenious ways. 'Visions of Enarc' was an extensive series in two phases lasting seven years. Courtesy © Barbara Crane, Chicago.

148 Brian Ogglesbee (American, b. 1951). Ogglesbee's studio-produced works are bizarre tableaux which combine elements of interior views, landscapes and still lifes in unlikely juxtapositions which aim to confound the viewer's normal expectations. In this image (which in the above sense is somewhat atypical), Ogglesbee has, so to speak, turned up the volume of the colour almost to the point of pain. Ogglesbee started as a commercial product photographer, mastering the manipulative techniques – both figuratively and literally speaking – which he now gleefully subverts. Courtesy Lieberman & Saul Gallery, New York; © Brian Ogglesbee.

149 Victor Landweber (American, b. 1943). Courtesy © Victor Landweber, Berkeley, California.

150 Tracey Holland (British, b. 1961). Holland's collage activities grew out of paintings of house fronts, old factories and other urban sites rendered in what she described as a 'fauvist style'. She then started building up the surface and this evolved naturally into collage. 'Instead of drawing the objects that fascinated me', she writes, 'I started instead to use them in the work. It was similar with photography. I stopped walking around for days trying to spot the perfectly composed photo and simply set up exactly what I wanted in the studio.'

Of this work she has written: 'In the *Incubus*, the onset of decay is hardly visible – the peony blossoms fall just at the peak of their perfection, revealing the picture's imperfection – the snake hidden in the centre.' Courtesy © Tracey Holland, Sheffield, England.

151 Ruth Thorne-Thomsen (American, b. 1943). Here is a quintessentially Symbolist artwork, heavy on symbols, obscure and ambiguous on meaning. Is this beautiful young woman (classically beautiful, like a Greek statue) in the process of becoming a flower, like the 19th-century *fleurs animées*. Or is she evolving *from* one? Is she real, or a phantom? And why the 'blindfold': to obscure the visible world in order to enhance her comprehension of it? Perhaps William Blake offers us a clue: 'Man's perceptions are not bounded by organs of perception, he perceives more than sense (tho' ever so acute) can discover.' Courtesy Ehlers Caudill Gallery, Chicago.

152 Vilem Kriz (Czech, naturalized American, b. 1921). Kriz has had a long association with the Surrealist movement, dating back to the 1940s when he lived and studied in Paris, but even before this he had been deeply influenced by the expressive and symbolist attitudes of Jaromir Funke and František Drtikol, his teachers and leading exponents of Czech photography (See 90). We see these unconventional ideas at play in this image: the pristine flower, its virtue at the mercy of occult forces. Courtesy Vilem Kriz, Berkeley, California, © 1979.

153, 154 Doug Prince (American, b. 1943). *Photosynthesis* is the botanical term for the process by which light energy is transformed into nourishment; 'Photosynthetics' therefore aptly describes Doug Prince's various kinds of two- and three-dimensional composite floral imagery. The first of these, of which two examples are shown here, are prints which have been made from single negatives, each of which is itself a combination of elements from two other negatives.

In the print series *Italian Observations*, for example, Prince marries individual flowers with aspects of medieval or Renaissance architecture – church and palace courtyards, domestic chambers, friezes, frescoes and the like. The composites are blended with great skill and sensitivity, so that the flowers and their foliage emerge 'naturally' from the architecture – or dissolve into it – the effect being not unlike an arrested film fade. Prince finds extraordinary correspondences between the man-made and the natural. Moreover, by inventing a means of fluidly combining disparate imagery he has extended the tradition of montage. Courtesy © Doug Prince; Witkin Gallery, New York.

155 Jerry Uelsmann (American, b. 1934). Some of Uelsmann's images are straightforward photographs. These are the ones, he has explained, which seem complete when he clicks the shutter. Others, however, are not complete; they are, so to speak, pieces of a puzzle which will later be fitted together. Uelsmann has described his contact sheets as store-houses of latent images, like seeds. At any time he might find the right image to be combined with another. In the darkroom, then, these seeds are nourished and brought to fruition through multiple printing techniques, negative printing and a number of other techniques Uelsmann has pioneered. His imagery reminds his viewer that 'the mind knows more than the eye and camera can see.' *See also 65*. Courtesy © Jerry Uelsmann, Gainesville, Florida.

156–59 Duane Michals (American, b. 1932). Since the 1960s Michals has been engaging his viewers with allegorical narrative sequences and paired imagery and text which question, on the one hand, the nature of 'the real' (the observed, the conceived, the dreamt, the believed, the disbelieved), and on the other, photograph's supposed capability, or claim, to capture these realities.

Whose dream is this? The subject's? The photographer's? What is, after all, 'real' in *A Dream of Flowers*? Apparently the flowers are not 'real' – they are dreamt. But would they be any more real for us, the viewers, if the sequence were called, say, *An Arrangement of Flowers*? Michals makes us aware of the *active* nature of seeing, the reciprocal relationship between seeing and what is seen. And is not photography itself a kind of dream? Like the Surrealists whom he reveres, Michals seeks the right questions rather than the right answers. Courtesy © Duane Michals, New York.

160 Eugène Atget (French, 1857–1927). Here Atget has given us a straightforward, naturalistic view of a bed of poppies quite unlike the artfully contrived Pictorialist visions of this period. Atget showed no interest in Pictorialism, finding the intrinsic properties of the medium sufficient scope for his descriptive, yet expressive, documentation. This particular image must be seen within the context of Atget's extensive study of the parks and gardens of Paris and environs, and this in turn within the context of his sweeping study of Paris. Courtesy Collection Stephen Shore, New York.

161 Denis Brihat (French, b. 1928). Over a period of ten years Brihat photographed a group of cherry trees in a small valley near his home in the south of France. Here he pays homage to one of these 'friends', as he came to think of them, with a tightly cropped study which vividly exhibits the tree's magnificent efflorescence. Only a small patch of black (bottom, centre) prevents the image from entirely metamorphosing into abstract pattern, with its calligraphic-like black markings. But as it stands, this borderline aspect is what gives us pleasure. *See also 63*. Courtesy © Denis Brihat, Bonnieux, France.

162 Stephen Shore (American, b.1947). In 1977 Shore, known for his superlative colour work, was commissioned by the Metropolitan Musuem and the *New York Times* to photograph Monet's gardens at Giverny; a selection of the prints was then used as introductory matter to the exhibition, *Monet's Years in Giverny*. Shore later received a futher commission from the *Reader's Digest* Foundation to follow the progress of the gardens as they were restored after forty years of neglect. The image shown here is from this latter period. Like Brihat, Shore fills the frame with flowers, dispensing with any distracting features such as paths, benches or ornament. Courtesy © Stephen Shore, New York.

163 Robert Walker (Canadian, b. 1943). For independent street photographer Robert Walker, always on the lookout for the unusual incident or the fleeting conjunction of disparate elements, the sight of a glowing, summery flower arrangement, briefly illuminated by the rays of the winter sun, was too hard to resist. Here was a ready-made 'flower-piece', framed not with mount and wood, but by icy reflections of cityscape and deep angular shadows. Like others of his generation, Walker has developed an expressive personal idiom of colour for his ongoing anthology of urban life. Courtesy © Robert Walker, Montreal.

164 Jerome Liebling (American, b. 1924). Liebling's picture provides 20th-century evidence of the flower's lasting symbolic potency, especially with regard to its role as a marker in *rites de passage*. On display in a shop window in Malaga, Liebling found a communion dress embroidered with a floral motif, next to which was a chaste arrangement of flowers in a vase. Particularly apt in symbolic terms is the lily, which seems to reach out to the dress; in Christianity, the lily stands for the Virgin Mary's purity. Courtesy © Jerome Liebling, Amherst, Massachusetts.

165 Albert Renger-Patzsch (German, 1897–1966). Courtesy Albin O. Kuhn Library and Gallery, University of Maryland, Baltimore County, © 1990.

166 Louis Faurer (American, b. 1916). *See also 53.* Courtesy © Louis Faurer, New York.

167 Ken Josephson (American, b. 1932). A more devastating critique of modern city living cannot be imagined. Nature has no place in Josephson's Chicago; even the sun is artificial. Yet for one harried citizen flowers obviously offer some form of solace; and judging from the *degree* of floral adornment one suspects that their force is even more potent, that perhaps of a talisman. Courtesy © Kenneth Josephson, Chicago.

168 Izis (Israëlis Bidermanas; Lithuanian, naturalized French, 1911–1980). Izis was enamoured of Paris, his adopted city since 1930. He delights his viewers with his gentle humour and his eye for the telling detail in otherwise unremarkable situations, detail which would be overlooked by a less sensitive vision. One such example is this modest arrangement brightening an otherwise drab Parisian windowsill. Like Walker and Josephson, Izis understood the deep spiritual need people expressed through such gestures. Courtesy National Gallery of Canada, Gift of Dorothy Meigs Eidlitz, St Andrews, New Brunswick, 1968.

169 Edward Weston (American, 1886–1958). When we think of Weston, we think not of flowers but of vegetable forms. But flowers were important to him; in his correspondence he often received pressed flowers from his friends. And as for photographs, there is a famous study of an orchid, which demonstrates that he did not find the subject daunting. Possibly, however, he felt that his friend and colleague Imogen Cunningham had claimed the territory. He was content to record flowers (or what was left of them after time had done its work) when he came across them, as here. Courtesy Leland Rice Collection; © 1981 Arizona Board of Regents, Centre for Creative Photography, Tucson, Arizona. *See also 183.*

170 Josef Sudek (Czech, 1896–1976). Prague was Sudek's main subject, although this could mean a view of a clothesline through a rain-streaked window as much as a sweeping panorama of the city's skyline. He was fascinated by the still life (*not* the 'nature morte', as nothing that interested him was truly dead!), but *this* could mean a rose-like jumble of rolled papers as much as a single white rose. For Sudek, one picture grew from another. Courtesy Collection Museum of Decorative Arts, Prague.

171 Lee Friedlander (American, b. 1934). Courtesy © Lee Friedlander; Laurence Miller Gallery, New York.

172 Edwin Smith (British, 1912–1971). Over his long and prolific career, which included the illustrations to more than twenty-five books, Smith demonstrated his deep affection for the English countryside, its buildings and gardens, and its people. Scenes of enchantment, such as the one shown here, are harder and harder to accept in the late 20th century — we would not be at all surprised to find that a shift of the camera by a few degrees would reveal an industrial plant, or a parking lot. Contemporary photographers would be hard pressed to find such an idyllic glade, at least in public land. Courtesy Mrs Edwin Smith, Saffron Walden, England.

173 Man Ray (American, 1890–1976). Man Ray's photograms and solarizations literally 'brought to light' a new photographic dimension. Like other Dadaists, he believed that a literal transcription of reality, the convincing reproduction of surface appearance, was in fact just another illusion, and that in order to break through to what was indeed 'real', the artist had to abandon realism and introduce a measure of abstraction. Pure abstraction, however, left the viewer without any contact with his own world. Man Ray was therefore always careful to anchor his imagery in the realm of recognizable objects, and flowers, such vivid emblems of the real world, were an ideal anchoring device. *See also 117.* Courtesy Timothy Baum Collection, New York.

174 Imogen Cunningham (American, 1883–1976). Man Ray (173) develops the theme of spiral and, by projecting an air of relaxation, conveys an *aura* rather than clinical detail. Cunningham, on the other hand, emphasizes the flower's alertness (almost animal in nature) and is very precise about texture and definition. The leaf, however, which in the Man Ray is clearly that — i.e., part of the plant — is treated here as something quite distinct from the flower, as a distant mountainscape or, without much taxing the imagination, a female breast. Cunningham had learned that a commitment to realism did not rule out symbolic form. *See also 58, 77.* Courtesy The Imogen Cunningham Trust, Berkeley, California.

175 Robert Mapplethorpe (American, 1946–1989). Whereas Cunningham's calla is alert and receptive, Mapplethorpe's is passive and demure, modestly acknowledging our admiration. Whereas Cunningham's thrusts upwards from the soil, Mapplethorpe's drops mysteriously from the sky — or, as it were, from the artist's imagination. Not for Mapplethorpe Ruskin's ideal of the flower in nature ('the most beautiful position in which flowers can be seen')! *See also 50, 60, 127, 134, 179.* Courtesy © The Estate of Robert Mapplethorpe, New York.

176 William Giles (American, b. 1934). With this bird's-eye-view Giles has chosen to somewhat subdue the flower itself in relation to its foliage, composing a rhythmic musical arrangement with the venation of the leaves and expecially with the highlights reflected by their edges. The image commemorates a significant moment in Giles's personal life; his mother was dying, and this revelation of nature's rhythms offered him solace. Courtesy © William Giles, Santa Fe, New Mexico.

177 Ansel Adams (American, 1902–1984). Courtesy The Trustees of the Ansel Adams Publishing Rights Trust, Carmel, California. All rights reserved.

178 Carlotta Corpron (American, 1901–1988). At opposite ends of the natural/artificial continuum from Giles, Corpron contrives an effective decorative arrangement, making good use of the solarization technique to define the flowers, which would otherwise (being more or less white on white) be lost in the background. Solarization as a phenomenon was known as early as the 1840s, but was not used for aesthetic purposes until the 1920s. Courtesy Amon Carter Museum, Forth Worth, Texas.

179 Robert Mapplethorpe (American, 1946–1989). *See also 50, 60, 127, 134, 175.* Courtesy © The Estate of Robert Mapplethorpe, New York.

180 Dr Dain Tasker (American, active c. 1930s). From the early 20th century, when soft X-rays made the photography of flowers possible, photographers were intrigued by the aesthetic as well as scientific potential of the technique. A better example cannot be imagined; Tasker has given us a lucid view of the flower's anatomy while making much of the magnificent swirl of the cornet. Courtesy Gordon L. Bennett Collection, Kentfield, California.

181 Chris Enos (American, b. 1944). The dead and decaying flower has not been much explored. Chris Enos is one of a handful of photographers who have found this terrain fruitful. Here she provides us with access to a world of wholly unfamiliar beauty. *See also 68.* Courtesy © Chris Enos, 1980, Boston.

182 Barbara Norfleet (American, b. 1926). Norfleet began to photograph dead or dying flowers around 1975, shortly after the death of her father. She had been unable to discard flowers sent to her in sympathy and found herself fascinated by how much their slow metamorphosis revealed of their inner structures. Their metamorphosis paralleled the sense of transition, rather than loss, that she felt at her father's death. She later produced a substantial body of work, from which the image is drawn. Courtesy © Barbara Norfleet, 1981, Cambridge, Massachusetts.

183 Edward Weston (American, 1886–1958). Weston's credo was 'rhythm, form and perfect detail', but this image seems to contain something more. Is there an allegorical intent? The spiral forms of lily and architectural ornament deliberately echo each other and everything appears less 'found' than arranged. Weston deliberately juxtaposes, even *opposes*, the debris of a worn-out culture to the freshness of the flower: fragile and 'fleeting' nature outshining the would-be permanence of the man-made. Courtesy International Museum of Photography at George Eastman House, Rochester, New York. 1981 Arizona Board of Regents, Centre for Creative Photography, Tucson, Arizona. *See also 169.*

Notes

1 Gail Buckland, *Fox Talbot and the Invention of Photography*, London, 1980, p. 19.

2 Ibid.

3 Ibid.

4 *Hermes – Or Classical and Antiquarian Researches*, London, 1838–9.

5 Kenneth Clark, *Landscape into Art*, Harmondsworth, Middlesex, 1949, p. 143.

6 Cited in Peter Mitchell, *Great Flower Painters: Four Centuries of Floral Art*, New York, 1973, p. 249.

7 John V. Brindle and James J. White, *Flora Portrayed*, Hunt Institute for Botanical Documentation, Carnegie-Mellon University, Pittsburgh, p. 41.

8 Ibid.

9 *See* Umberto Baldini, *Primavera: The Restoration of Botticelli's Masterpiece*, New York, 1986, pp. 101–108.

10 Gerrit van Spaendonck was the first flower painter to favour transparent watercolour over opaque, and the first to adapt a stipple process of etched dots in the reproductive process.

11 Peter Mitchell (Note 6), p. 236.

12 *See* André Jammes and Eugenia Parry Janis, *The Art of French Calotype*, Princeton, New Jersey, 1983.

13 Brindle and White (Note 7), p. 48.

14 Cited in Naomi Rosenblum, 'Adolphe Braun: A 19th-Century Career in Photography', *History of Photography* 3 (October 1979): 370.

15 The technical obstacles Braun had to overcome were daunting: the glassplates were exposed in sunlight over half-hour periods, and the effect of the wind and the natural wilting would have taken their toll. *See* Rosenblum (Note 14).

16 Anne McCauley, 'Photographs for Industry: The Career of Charles Aubry,' *J. P. Getty Museum Journal* 14 (1986): 163.

17 Bibliothèque Nationale, Paris, Etude de Feuilles, Ire Série, signed dedication by Aubry, 31 May, 1864. Quoted in McCauley (Note 16), p. 159.

18 'Three hundred to four hundred million *cartes* were estimated to be sold annually in England at the height of the carte-de-visite period,' notes Helmut Gernsheim in *The Rise of Photography, 1850–1880*, London, 1989, p. 201.

19 These conventions also characterized larger formats of portraiture, such as the Imperial, Boudoir and Promenade.

20 In many cases, *The Photographic News* of April, 1976, informs us, 'The grouping surrounds a scroll containing some lines of poetry, or a collect from the Book of Common Prayer. In other cases the flowers are grouped so as to form a cross' (p. 199).

21 *Gibson's General Catalogue*, No. 21, n.d., The Gibson Photo Jewelry Company, Brooklyn, New York. Courtesy Olivia Parker, Manchester, Massachussetts.

22 James Mew, 'Photographic Botany', *The Photographic News*, April, 1892, p. 259.

23 Edward Aveling, 'Botany and Photography', *The Photographic News*, March, 1892, p. 197.

24 Quoted in James Mew (Note 22), p. 260.

25 James Mew (Note 22), p. 260.

26 Edward Aveling (Note 23), p. 197.

27 James Mew (Note 22), p. 259. But *The British Journal of Photography*, of 27 May, 1887, agreed that colour was far off. An anonymous correspondent was quoted: 'It is needless in these days, when a scientific primer can be bought for one shilling, to point out the boastful absurdity and inherent nonsense of any pretensions to photograph colours directly. To do so would be to attempt to rival the exploits of those wise old gentlemen of Laputa whom Lemuel Gulliver discovered engaged in the process of extracting sunbeams from cucumbers' (p. 371).

28 Originally, nature printing, a Renaissance invention, was accomplished with the plant itself, which was inked and served as the plate. By the 19th century the process was considerably refined.

29 *Athenaeum*, 6 April, 1839.

30 Atkins explained to readers of her 1843 *British Algae: Cyanotype Impressions*, that it was 'the difficulty of making accurate drawings of objects as minute as many of the Algae and Confera [which] has induced me to avail myself of Sir John Herschel's beautiful process of Cyanotype . . .' Cited in Larry J. Schaaf, *Sun Gardens*, New York, 1985, p. 8.

31 27 April, 1892, p. 260.

32 'Photographing Flowers', *The British Journal of Photography*, 20 May, 1887, p. 305.

33 Ibid.

34 *The Photographic News*, July, 1888, p. 423.

35 Robert Offord, 'Floral Photography', *The Photographic News*, July, 1885, p. 484.

36 Ibid.

37 'Photographing Flowers' (Note 32), p. 306.

38 Ibid. p. 322. The journal advises: 'As a rough idea, we may mention that at a distance of three or four feet from a window about four feet by three feet in dimensions, and facing south, we are in the habit of giving them three to fifteen minutes . . .'

39 'Photographing Flowers' (Note 32), p. 305.

40 Cited in James Mew (Note 22), p. 259.

41 Cited in Peter Bunnell, ed., *A Photographic Vision: Pictorial Photography 1889–1923*, Salt Lake City, Utah, 1980, p. 21.

42 Sadakichi Hartmann, 'F. Holland Day, A Decorative Photographer', in Harry W. Lawton and George Knox, *The Valiant Knights of Daguerre*, Berkeley, California, 1978, p. 188.

43 Dennis Longwell, *Steichen, The Master Prints 1895–1914*, New York, 1978, p. 174.

44 Cecil Beaton and Gail Buckland, *The Magic Image*, London, 1975, p. 106.

45 Carl Sandburg, *Steichen the Photographer*, New York, 1929, p. 36.

46 Cited in David Mellor, ed., *Germany: The New Photography 1927–33*, London, 1978, pp. 17–19.

47 Cited in Naomi Rosenblum, *A World History of Photography*, New York, 1984, p. 392.

48 Although Man Ray believed he had invented, or discovered, the photogram, it had actually been invented by Fox Talbot and Hippolyte Bayard. Moreover, Christian Schad and László Moholy-Nagy made the discovery simultaneously with Man Ray.

49 Christopher Dresser, *Art of Decorative Design*, London, 1862.

50 Owen Jones, *The Grammar of Ornament*, London, 1856, p. 5.

51 Cited in McCauley (Note 16), p. 168.

52 Cited in Ray Desmond, 'A Surfeit of Nature', *The British Museum Book of Flowers*, London, 1989, p. 132.

53 Cited in Volker Kahmen, *Ernst Fuhrmann*, exhibition catalogue, Galerie Rudolph Kicken, Cologne, 1979, p. 49.

54 Cited in Van Deren Coke, *Avant Garde Photography in Germany 1919–1939*, San Francisco, 1980, p. 21.

55 Albert Renger-Patzsch, 'Ziele', *Das Deutsche Lichtbild, 1927*, p. 18.

56 Volker Kahmen (Note 53), pp. 46–51.

57 Theodore E. Stebbins, Jr., and Norman Keyes, Jr., *Charles Sheeler: The Photographs*, Boston, 1987, p. 4.

58 Ed. Elaine Dines, in collaboration with Graham Howe, *Paul Outerbridge, A Singular Aesthetic*, catalogue raisonné, Laguna Beach Museum of Art, California, 1981, p. 15.

59 Ibid. pp. 33–34.

60 Edward Weston, *Daybooks*, Vol. 2, p. 154, 1930.

61 Edward Weston had reviewed Cunningham's exhibition at a Carmel gallery with the following accolade: 'She uses her medium, photography, with honesty – no tricks, no evasion: a clean cut presentation of the thing itself . . .' Quoted in Richard Lorenz, *Imogen Cunningham: Frontiers*, catalogue, Imogen Cunningham Trust, Berkeley, California, 1978, n.p.

62 Heather Alberts, 'Konrad Cramer: A Woodstock Photographer', *Image* 29 (January 1986): 3.

63 John W. N. Sullivan, 'X-Ray Photographs of Flowers', *Scientific American*, 27 June, 1914, p. 523.

64 D. L. Tasker, 'X-Ray Goes Pictorial', *Popular Photography*, March, 1842, pp. 78–79.

65 R. H. Noailles, *The Hidden Life of Flowers*, trs. J. M. Guilcher, London, 1954.

66 In correspondence with the author, July, 1990.

67 Cited in Rod Slemmons, *Like a One-Eyed Cat: Photographs by Lee Friedlander*, New York, 1989, p. 115.

68 Cited in Naomi Rosenblum, *A World History of Photography*, New York, p. 585.

69 Pierre Boogaerts, 'AN INVESTIGATION OF THE PHOTOGRAPHIC RECTANGLE, THE INTERIOR AS WITH THE EXTERIOR, AND OF MY WORKING METHODS. AND WITH SEVERAL DETOURS ALONG THE WAY . . .', *Anamnèse*, Montreal, 1989, p. 71.

70 Cited in Lise Lamarche, 'REMEMBERING ARAGO OR THE MISPLACED READER', *Anamnèse*, Montreal, 1989, p. 52.

71 John Ruskin, *The Crown of Wild Olive*, Philadelphia, 1895, p. 19.

Acknowledgments

The works presented in *Flora Photographica* are drawn from a wide variety of sources, including museums, libraries, galleries, public and private collections, and the photographers themselves. I must thank first and foremost the contemporary photographers who have contributed their work to this enterprise and who supported my efforts to organize this anthology:

John Atchley, Gordon L. Bennett, Pierre Boogaerts, Denis Brihat, Carlotta Corpron, Barbara Crane, Jean Dieuzaide, Gerald Ducimetière, Chris Enos, Louis Faurer, Joan Fontcuberta, Lee Friedlander, Marvin Gasoi, William Giles, Jan Groover, Betty Hahn, Rick Hock, Tracey Holland, Dennis Hopper, Eikoh Hosoe, Yasuhiro Ishimoto, Stefan De Jaeger, Ken Josephson, E.F. Kitchen, Vilem Kriz, Victor Landweber, Cay Lang, David Lebe, Helen Levitt, Jerome Liebling, Steve Lovi, Sally Mann, Sheila Metzner, Joel Meyerowitz, Duane Michals, Arnold Newman, Barbara Norfleet, Brian Ogglesbee, Suzanne Opton, Olivia Parker, Doug Prince, Dr Albert G. Richards, Lucas Samaras, Stephen Shore, Michael Spano, Doug and Mike Starn, Bert Stern, John Stezaker, Elisabeth Sunday, Keiichi Tahara, Ruth Thorne-Thomsen, Jerry Uelsmann, Raymond Voinquel, Robert Walker, Don Worth.

I am deeply grateful for the assistance of curatorial staff at the following institutions:

The Addison Gallery of American Art, Andover, Massachusetts; The Royal Photographic Society, Bath; Alma Lavenson Associates, Berkeley, California; The Imogen Cunningham Trust, Berkeley, California; Bibliothèque Royale Albert 1e, Brussels; The Polaroid Collection, Cambridge, Massachusetts; Ansel Adams Publishing Rights Trust, Carmel, California; The Art Institute of Chicago; Columbia College, Chicago; Field Museum of Natural History, Chicago; Agfa Foto Historama, Cologne; Museum Ludwig, Cologne; Museum Folkwang, Essen; Amon Carter Museum, Fort Worth, Texas; Hallmark Photographic Collection, Hallmark Cards, Kansas City, Missouri; The J. Paul Getty Museum, Malibu, California; Albin O. Kuhn Library and Gallery, University of Maryland, Baltimore County; Paul Strand Archive, Aperture Foundation Inc., Millerton, New York; Minneapolis Institute of Arts, Minneapolis; New Orleans Museum of Art; Estate of André

Kertész, New York; Estate of Robert Mapplethorpe, New York; Gilman Paper Company Collection, New York; The Museum of Modern Art, New York; The New York Public Library; The Oakland Museum, Oakland, California; The National Gallery of Canada, Ottawa; Bibliothèque Nationale, Paris; Société Française de Photographie, Paris; Curatorial Assistance, Pasadena, California; Hunt Institute for Botanical Documentation, Carnegie-Mellon University, Pittsburgh, Pennsylvania; Museum of Decorative Arts, Prague; International Museum of Photography at George Eastman House, Rochester, New York; San Francisco Museum of Modern Art; Schaffer Library, Union College, Schenectady, New York; August Sander Archive, Sinsig, Germany; Center for Creative Photography, Tucson, Arizona; Worcester Art Museum, Worcester, Massachusetts; Karl Blossfeldt Archive, Zülpich, Germany.

I owe a special debt to the enthusiastic collectors who brought key or unusual works to my attention:

Palmquist Collection, Arcata, California (Peter E. Palmquist); Leland Rice Collection, Berkeley, California; Gordon L. Bennett Collection, Kentfield, California; Leonard and Marjorie Vernon Collection, Los Angeles, California; John and Olivia Parker Collection, Manchester, Massachusetts; Tim Baum Collection, New York; Uwe Scheid Collection, Uberherrn/Saar, Germany.

The following galleries graciously lent prints and transparencies for the project:

Lee Gallery, Boston; William L. Schaeffer, Chester, Connecticut; Edwynn Houk Gallery, Chicago; Ehlers Caudill Gallery, Chicago; Kicken/Pauseback Gallery, Cologne; Anthony d'Offay Gallery, London; Kate Heller Gallery, London; Salama-Caro Gallery, London; G. Ray Hawkins Gallery, Los Angeles; L. A. Louver, Los Angeles; Laurence Miller Gallery, New York; Robert Miller Gallery, New York; Lieberman & Saul Gallery, New York; Pace/MacGill Gallery, New York; Photofind, New York; Brent Sikkema Fine Arts, New York; Staley/Wise Gallery, New York; Stux Gallery, New York; The Witkin Gallery, New York; Zabriskie

Gallery, New York/Paris; Fraenkel Gallery, San Francisco; Jane Corkin Gallery, Toronto.

David Spear and Sal Lopes are owed thanks for their superb copy prints made when original materials could not be loaned. They sometimes worked from material in less than pristine condition. Karen Miksche provided invaluable research assistance.

Lastly, I want to thank the following individuals who offered support or advice, pointed the way to interesting work, or provided vital information:

Robert Alter, Pierre Apraxine, Gordon Baldwin, Els Barents, Nancy Barrett, Timothy Baum, Tom Beck, Deborah Bell, Gordon L. Bennett, James Borcoman, Jan Buerger, Marty Carey, Shashi Caudill, Michèle Chomette, Denise Colomb, Jane Corkin, Nina Cummings, Evelyne Z. Daitz, Keith Davis, Robert Dean, Priska Dissel, Susan Ehrens, James Enyeart, John Falconer, David Featherstone, Pamela Feld, Barbara Galasso, Helen Gee, Howard Greenberg, Thomas D. Grischkowsky, Claudia M. Gropper, Robert Gurbo, Nell Guttman, Julie van Haften, G. Ray Hawkins, Debra Heimer-Dinger, Beatrice Helg, Therese Heyman, Barbara Hitchcock, Francis Hodgson, Graham Howe, Edwynn Houk, Deborah Ireland, Madame Izis, Ken Jacobson, Margaret E. Kelly, Rudi Kicken, Zdenek Kirschner, Susan Kismaric, Robert Knodt, Ken Jacobson, Stephen Jareckie, Brooks Johnson, Kathleen Lamb, Hugh and Jane LeBaron, Mack Lee, Jean-Claude Lemagny, Anne Longdon, Bernard Marbot, Lee Marks, Bernard McTigue, David Mellor, Laurence Miller, Rheinhold Misselbeck, Anthony Montoya, Weston Naef, Julia Nelson-Gal, Peter E. Palmquist, John and Olivia Parker, Ron and Elizabeth Partridge, Anne Pasternak, Sylvain Pelly, Marcuse Pfeiffer, Terence Pitts, Leland Rice, Pam Roberts, Christiane Roger, Grant Romer, Gerd Sander, Julie Saul, William L. Schaeffer, Uwe Scheid, James Sheldon, Ruth Silverman, Mrs Olive Smith, Ethaline Staley, Dominique Stoops, Tina Summerlin, Ann Thomas, Tony Troncale, Anne Tucker, Ellen Ushioka, Jeanne Verhulst, Leonard and Marjorie Vernon, Robert Walker, Mike Weaver, Colin Westerbeck, James J. White, Stephen White, Ann and Jürgen Wilde, Taki Wise, Sylvia Wolf, David Wooters, Virginia Zabriski.

Photographic Acknowledgments

Courtesy Rijksmuseum, Amsterdam: p. 8 (bottom); Courtesy The Royal Photographic Society, Bath: pp. 16, 18; Courtesy © The Imogen Cunningham Trust, Berkeley, California: p. 24 (top); Courtesy Susan Ehrens, Berkeley, California, © Alma Lavenson Associates: p. 24 (bottom); Courtesy Leland Rice Collection, Berkeley, California: pp. 6, 14; Courtesy Denis Brihat, Bonnieux, France: pp. 2–3; Courtesy © 1990 The Art Institute of Chicago. All rights reserved. Gift of Harold Allen, 1976. 1070. Originally published by Strubmeyer and Wyman: p. 13 (top); Courtesy © 1990 The Art Institute of Chicago. All rights reserved. The Julian

Levy Collection, Gift of Jean Levy and the Estate of Julian Levy, 1988; p. 26 (bottom); Courtesy Edwynn Houk Gallery, Chicago: p. 26 (top); Courtesy Gordon L. Bennett Collection, Kentfield, California: p. 12 (bottom); Courtesy Salama-Caro Gallery, London, © John Stezaker, London: p. 9 (bottom); Courtesy Leonard and Marjorie Vernon, Los Angeles, California: p. 20; Courtesy The J. Paul Getty Museum, Malibu, California: p. 19; Courtesy Olivia and John Parker, Manchester, Massachusetts: pp. 13 (bottom), 15; Courtesy © 1971, Aperture Foundation Inc., Paul Strand Archive, Millerton, New York: p. 27 (bottom);

Courtesy Gilman Paper Company Collection, New York: p. 23; Courtesy © The Estate of Robert Mapplethorpe, New York: p. 28; Courtesy The Oakland Museum, Oakland, California: p. 1; Courtesy The National Gallery of Canada, Ottawa: p. 17; Courtesy Bibliothèque Nationale, Paris: pp. 10 (top, bottom), 11, 12 (top); Courtesy Hunt Institute for Botanical Documentation, Carnegie-Mellon University, Pittsburgh, Pennsylvania: pp. 7, 8 (top), 9 (top); Courtesy Karl Blossfeldt Archive, Ann and Jürgen Wilde, Zülpich, Germany.

Index

Page numbers in *italic* refer to the illustrations; numbers in **bold** refer to the plates